Coping With Food Intolerances

SURVIVING THE NINETIES

Dick Thom, D.D.S., N.D.

JELD Publications ❧ Portland, Oregon

IMPORTANT

The information in this book is not intended to replace the services of a physician or other qualified medical counseling. The purpose of this book is to educate. If you are sick, you should see a physician. This book is sold with the understanding that the author and publisher are not liable for the misconception or misuse of information provided. Every effort has been made to make this book as complete and as accurate as possible. The author and publisher shall have neither liability nor responsibility to any person or entity with respect to any loss, damage, or injury caused or alleged to be caused directly or indirectly by the information contained in this book.

Editing by Paul Bergner
Copy editing by Eileen Ridge
Typography and production by Bergner Communications
Cover design and illustrations by Becky Morrell

ISBN 0-9631918-1-0

Library of Congress Catalog Card Number
95-81909

For information or ordering contact:

JELD Publications
Beaverton Center for the Healing Arts
4720 S.W. Watson Avenue
Beaverton, OR 97005
(503) 526-0397

Printed in the United States of America

Acknowledgements

I would like to thank my teachers, especially Dr. Steve Austin, who remains a continual inspiration to me to keep researching the concepts of food intolerance, and to all those who have written about the health problems associated with food sensitivities. I have learned much from your work.

A very special thank you to my devoted students and patients whose thoughtful questions, comments and reprints prompted me to rewrite this book with its many additions.

My family has continued to give much to allow me to spend time to research and record this information. To my children, Julie and Eric, and my lovely wife, Lise, a heartfelt thank you for your sacrifices. I have spent many late nights working with your wonderful understanding. Thanks.

I would like to dedicate this book to all the patients who are willing to assume self-responsibility for their own health and are searching out the means for achieving it. Congratulations.

Table of Contents

Foreword

Allergies to inhalants, contactants, and ingestants are disturbing, irritating, frustrating, and sometimes expensive. Most of us have a few; some of us have many. Some of us know what things bother us and what to avoid. Many of us know there is something wrong, but cannot pinpoint the specific offender. A few of us are surly, tired, sickly and miserable, but many have no idea that allergies can produce all the symptoms, many of which appear to be psychosomatic. To a certain extent, the existence of the allergy is an opportunity for the victim to do something about his lifestyle. There is something wrong and the sooner some attention is paid to the allergy, other diseases and conditions lying dormant around the corner may never emerge.

Allergies mean the immune system is injured. The sooner it is repaired, the less the chance that the body will slip into some other more devastating condition: cancer, addiction, depression, obesity — the list goes on. Hay fever may turn into asthma. Gas and dyspepsia could turn into Crohn's disease or ulcerative colitis. The body is trying to help by sending signals to the owner. It is saying "Pay attention; if you cannot believe this nose bleed is a dairy allergy, I'll give you a migraine."

Dr. Thom leads us through the complexities of inhalant allergies and food sensitivities with clarity and linearity. He gives the reader insight into the mechanism of the various types of allergies. But he does not leave us with "Just drink water, and you will be okay." He provides the sufferer with a host of adequate substitutes to fill the gaps when one must leave out the big five: wheat, corn, dairy, soy and egg.

Most people who suffer from allergies have some genetic tendency, but the actual allergic symptoms did not show up until some stress, injury or actual sickness acted as the trigger. Some people get better as they age; some get worse. An acid/base balance tilt might have allowed the allergy to surface. The stress of the allergy on the system can exhaust the adrenal glands, trying to produce enough hormones to control the problem, so the sensitivity becomes a vicious cycle. The allergy sufferer cannot get well because he is allergic.

If one restricts his diet to water, sweet potatoes, squash, fish, and millet, he may temporarily reduce his allergic symptoms, but his body will be unable to regain control because it does not get enough nutrients to shore up the flagging immune system. Most allergic people are deficient in a number of nutrients, such as vitamins C, B6, B3, pantothenic acid and the minerals calcium and magnesium. Allergic people need all the help they can get. Dr. Thom offers the latest ideas in diagnosis, testing and diet substitutions.

Standard MD allergists are doing the best they can, but the "science" of allergology has not advanced much in the last twenty-five years. It is said that intelligent people are more likely to have allergies. It may be that only intelligent people are smart enough to realize that something is wrong, and it is not just the roll of the dice.

I used to take care of a girl who developed a high fever and pus in her urine if she drank an ounce of milk. The mother figured that one out. "Every time Melissa drinks milk, she gets a fever and a kidney infection." I scoffed until she proved it to me. About 60% of bedwetters wet the bed because they are eating or drinking something to which they are sensitive. The same statistics apply to ear infections; they will not clear up until the offending food has been stopped. The *Lancet,* the British medical journal, printed a study several years ago that showed 93% of migraines were triggered by a food intolerance. Anything can do anything. If a symptom or a disease does not make sense, think of a sensitivity. Do not assume that if the cause of something is vague, it has to be a psychiatric condition.

The incidence of sensitivities is increasing, Dr. Thom points out, because our modern diets do not provide the nutrients we need to help strengthen our immune system, but also because we are eating the same foods over and over again.

He didn't say it, but he implies that we should go back to the diets of our ancestors who lived in the hunting and gathering days two million to twenty million years ago: much raw food, very little fat, fruits and vegetables in season, a smidgen of honey, but no milk and hardly any grains.

Thank you, Dr. Thom, for your insights.

You may think you do not have allergies. You will be surprised to find that you probably do. Here is the book to unravel the mystery of your sensitivities and what to do about them, and at the same time, bolster your immune system, so some other disease won't catch you.

Lendon Smith, M.D.

Preface to the first edition

Our food choices are very personal, and for many of us they've been with us since childhood. We now commonly eat foods which we grew to like as we were raised. Your parents' dietary habits are likely reflected in what you commonly eat. In my practice I have observed many patients improve their health when they decided to make dietary changes. These changes were usually very challenging and difficult at first.

At first, I had little information to give them, other than suggesting several books. For most people this was time-consuming and did not prove to be very effective.

As time went on, I decided to provide them with more written information, so they could read in one place dietary information suited specifically for them. This enabled them to make wise choices in their food intake. This seemed to enhance their ability to follow the dietary recommendations I was making.

I have been asked by many people to make these suggestions available to other people. This book is an effort to provide you with some basic suggestions for making dietary changes.

Food intolerance remains a difficult problem to evaluate but changes in new technology are very encouraging. I have been doing some research in this area and hope that in the near future, many people will have access to quick, painless and effective methods of food intolerance evaluation.

As you read through this book, I encourage you to try new foods, new recipes and break away from your old dietary habits.

Good luck as you search out personal growth and health enhancement through dietary changes.

September 1991
D.W. Thom, D.D.S., N.D.

Preface to second edition

After the first printing of the book, I received a lot of comments and questions about certain aspects of food sensitivities. I have attempted to clarify some points in this edition and have added several new chapters, including ones which discuss the common hay-fever type allergies and the importance of breast feeding.

Additional recipes have been included and I tried to reorganize the information so it will be of more practical value. I hope you find these changes useful as you pursue a higher level of wellness. As always, your comments and questions are greatly appreciated.

March, 1992
D. W. Thom, D.D.S., N.D.

Preface to the third edition

The field and science of food intolerance is growing at a rapid rate. Four years ago there was little acceptance in the concept of food intolerances. Conventional medicine and the media are changing their mind as more information about the diet and essential nutrients are being published on a daily/weekly basis.

More and more specialists, including pediatricians, cardiologists, urologists, pulmonologists and internists are looking beyond their usual scope of therapeutic ideas and starting to address the issue that food choices are directly linked to many chronic health problems.

I continue to be amazed by the thirst for knowledge that the general population has for self-health improvement. A study last year demonstrated that there were more patient visits in alternative health care than there were in conventional medicine. Patients are beginning to realize there are no magic bullets and health can only be achieved by hard work and perseverance. I have expanded the text to include more helpful information for everyday food choices. The shopping list and menu ideas should help you get a start on food substitutions. Once you have mastered these foods and include them routinely in your diet, you will be well on your way to a level of health you rightly deserve.

Please use this book as a reference text. There is a lot information and I have tried to organize it for ease of use.

Congratulations on your sincere desire for health optimization.

December 1995
Dick Thom D.D.S., N.D.

Chapter One

Allergies, Intolerances, Irritants and Your Health

Allergies are sensitivities to substances which the majority of people find harmless. By definition, an allergy involves an immunologic reaction between an antigen (example: food, chemical, inhalant) and an antibody produced in the body. Food intolerances and irritants provoke reactions through other mechanisms, and are far more common than many people believe. No one doubts that food allergies exist, but for many in conventional medical circles, the existence and frequency of non-allergic food intolerances are controversial.

Food allergy

The term *food allergy* is often used erroneously to describe what are actually food intolerances. The reason for the confusion is the poor definition of the terms. When people develop antibodies against a food, the food becomes an allergen, and a true allergy exists. Lessof, Wraith and their co-authors have suggested the term *food allergy* should be restricted to patients who have immediate allergic reactions to specific food or foods, together with evidence of specific antibody IgE in the form of positive skin prick tests or radio allergo sorbent tests (RAST). Most reactions to food do not involve this classic antigen-antibody reaction; therefore, traditional allergists are skeptical that food can cause a wide variety of problems for many individuals. Most allergists believe that only a few people have food allergies, with a short list of foods which cause only a few possible symptoms. These symptoms include urticaria (hives), anaphylaxis (an emergency situation where the windpipe closes), rhinitis (runny nose) and stomach problems. In the case of allergy,

1

the antibodies may be detected in the blood by conventional testing so it is considered a specific and detectable condition.

Food intolerance

The term *food intolerance* is a much broader term than food allergy. It includes many types of problems which may be correlated with any food. These are not the classical antibody-antigen reactions described above and therefore they do not show up on conventional allergy testing. For this reason, some physicians questions their existence. Only after careful observation and detective work can the underlying effects of many foods be uncovered.

Food irritants

In the past year I have chosen to refer to these non-specific food reactions/intolerances as *food irritants* rather than food intolerances. Throughout this book I will refer interchangeably to the terms food intolerances and food irritants.

Food and immunity

I believe intolerant foods have an irritating effect on the body which ultimately weakens the immune system. One of the best ways to enhance your immune system is to reduce your daily exposure to irritating foods, and substitute better-tolerated foods. Emphasis must also be placed on building health using therapies which can aid and strengthen the immune system.

A common problem?

Over 35 million people in the U.S. suffer at some time from known allergies, ranging from mild to severe. Allergies, intolerances and irritants are among the most prevalent causes of illness in the U.S. The following statistics were compiled by the National Institute of Allergy and Infectious Diseases:

* Eight percent of children under 6 years old experience food allergies while 1-2% of adults are believed to be sensitive.

* Allergy testing was listed as the reason for 1.4 million office visits to physicians in 1991.

* Hay fever affects 8% of men and 12% of women and was the reason for 9.4 million office visits in 1991. The cost of treatment is estimated at over $1.8 billion.

* Allergic reactions are the most common skin condition in children under 11 years old.

* Hives and swollen throat tissue affect 15% of the U.S. population annually.

* Chronic sinusitis, commonly caused by allergies, affects nearly 36.6 million people in the U.S.

* The number of cases of asthma is steadily rising, with a reported 12.4 million people, including 4.2 million children, in 1992.

The statistics are beginning to reach staggering proportions. The number of substances (food and environmental) to which people are exposed has gone up dramatically in the last few decades. Some of the foods we consume most often are foreign to us, in terms of our genetic backgrounds. For example, soy and corn were not eaten in Europe, where the majority of Americans have their genetic roots.

Recently a mother brought her ten-year-old daughter to my office because the child was having a number of health problems which included intolerable mood changes. It had been assumed for years it was a part of her personality. After making some dietary changes which included the exclusion of corn, the re-introduction of popcorn in the diet caused a return of moodiness and irritability that had disappeared for weeks. The effect of eating the popcorn lasted more than three days.

Common symptoms

Intolerances can affect any organ system of the body. They may cause rhinitis, breathing problems, digestive problems, itching skin, hives, eczema, rash, headaches, insomnia, hyper-irritability, anxiety, depression, and concentration problems. While intolerances are not responsible for all health problems, they are important to consider when other investigations have been unsuccessful in uncovering the cause of a problem.

Wouldn't I know if I had food sensitivities?

This is a commonly asked question. This is similar to the cigarette smoker who has lung problems but doesn't know it. Most people have lost or forgotten the signal which the body initially gave them when ingesting an irritant food. Just as watery eyes, nausea and excessive saliva are common the first time a person smokes a cigarette, the body eventually gives up trying to provide an early warning system. The person continues to smoke and in fact learns to feel even more satisfied for indulging in this toxic behavior.

The dynamics of food sensitivities is similar. Long ago the body gave up on colic, ear aches, colds, headaches, itchy skin and now the body seems to even crave the very food which is causing internal dysfunction. It is not until one or more systems have become more seriously dysfunctional that the body makes another attempt to let you know that there are problems. Please remember that all symptoms are important attempts by the body to communicate and provide direction for the mind in response to dysfunction. They are signals for change.

Why me?

The combination of exposure to the offending agent, genetics, and health at time of exposure influences the development of an overly sensitive immune system and development of food sensitivities.

Choose your parents well!

Children can become sensitized to foods before they are born. Studies have shown that overeating of some food(s) by the mother during pregnancy leads to sensitivities in the child. If both your parents have allergies, you have a 70% chance of following suit. If only one parent has an allergy, 30-60% of children will develop an allergy. However, it does not have to be the same allergy that your parent(s) had. If your mother smoked while she was pregnant, you have four times the risk of anyone else for developing an allergy — whether or not you also have a family history of allergy.

Food sensitivity and age

Many people tend to believe that food sensitivities occur only among children or infants, who experience vomiting or stomach aches after eating. Adults don't expect to become sensitive and commonly believe that any childhood sensitivities disappear with age. However, nothing could be further from the truth. The older you get the more likely you are to develop the symptoms of food sensitivity.

In a general family practice I see patients of all ages. The two-day-old babies I see who are breast feeding but have terrible colic are sensitized to a food their mother is eating. The ninety-two year-old great-grandmother couldn't believe the coffee she drank for eighty years could possibly be related to her daily heartburn. It was!

The newborn

During the time immediately after birth and weaning the human organism is particularly susceptible to exposure and development of sensitivities. Being born or weaned during or immediately prior to the peak season of pollen increases the risk of sensitization to a particular allergen. This has been shown for grass, birch, and ragweed allergies. If you are exposed to cow's milk at any time in the first six months of life, (including breast milk if your mother was drinking cow's milk), you're more likely to be sensitive to it than someone who had no exposure in those early months of life. In fact, in Sweden's hospital nurseries, nurses are not permitted to give cow's milk to infants without a doctor's prescription!

Are allergies ever outgrown?

Many people are led to believe their children will outgrow any allergies they may have. However, this frequently is not the case. Common childhood allergy symptoms include earache, tonsillitis, colic, eczema and respiratory problems. They may indeed outgrow their childhood allergies only to develop more serious, "deeper" problems later in life. For example, infantile eczema may later become bronchial asthma or some form of gastrointestinal problem. The sensitivity just moves from one organ system to another.

I remember one distraught young mother in her late twenties who said she could not cope anymore. Depression, PMS, and caring for two young children seemed overwhelming. Her past included a history of colic, ear infections, asthma and migraine headaches. Removing dairy products from her diet changed her life.

Air pollution

Another factor to consider is air pollution. There has been an increase in allergies in industrialized nations. It is not that you are allergic to the pollution itself, but rather the pollutants — primarily tobacco smoke, nitrogen dioxide, ozone, and sulphur dioxide — prime the immune system and you are more likely to be sensitive. It appears also that if you do not have a family history of allergies, the pollutants do not seem to have the same effect.

Frequency of exposure and allergic load

The more often a person is exposed to a specific kind of food, the more he or she is likely to be prone to sensitivity. Too much exposure to one kind of food may overwhelm the immune system and trigger the sensitivity response. The combined assault of chemicals, excessive pollens, dusts, and molds with too much milk, wheat, corn, chocolate, coffee, MSG, or sugar can overload the resistance system to the breaking point.

Variety is the spice of life

Other than heredity, the most common reason for sensitivity is the lack of variety in the diet. Because of the obsession with speeding up and simplifying food preparation, "fast food" items have taken over meal planning. The typical diet is more and more repetitious — eating dairy, wheat, corn, soy, tomatoes, coffee, wine, beer and sugar over and over. With such eating habits, it is not surprising that anyone can develop food sensitivities. The only difference from person to person is the timing of the appearance of sensitivities and the specific symptoms when they do appear. This suggests that, unless we make changes, at some point virtually everyone will experience some level of food sensitivity.

I have done numerous studies of the number of foods people tend to eat on a routine basis. Thirty foods or less is very common. Patients eating the fewest number of foods are likely to experience the most problems. I have seen patients eating as few as four foods only and they wondered why they had health problems which commonly included fatigue and headaches.

Other problems

A person's degree of susceptibility may also depend on metabolic factors such as increased or decreased thyroid activity, adrenal insufficiency and hypoglycemia (low blood sugar). People taking antibiotics may develop food intolerances (Hunter

7

et al.). An extensive study of women who received antibiotics after a hysterectomy frequently developed irritable bowel syndrome (IBS) (alternating diarrhea/constipation, cramps). The bacteria in the intestines were different from those women who had not developed the problem. This suggests that the antibiotics kill various types of bacteria in the intestine and allow other types to develop. These bacteria react differently during digestion which results in the IBS condition.

Sensitivities involve a dysfunctioning of the immune system. Perhaps all the stresses and unnatural lifestyles many of us live with could be changing the immune system's ability to cope with antigens. Symptoms develop when people exceed the threshold of their intolerance. Thus eliminating foods to which you are sensitive may allow you to tolerate environmental allergens (pollens, dust, animal dander etc.). This may partly explain why a person may react to a food one time and not another. Many people have a wheat sensitivity only during the grass pollen season; and as a corollary, if they eat no wheat in the spring, they may not have hay fever when they mow the lawn.

Withdrawal and delayed reactions

Most people who are sensitive to food are unaware of it because the reaction may be delayed for many hours after ingestion. In addition, the reaction may last for many days. If a food has not been eaten for some time and then is ingested, a reaction may happen fairly quickly. If a person is sensitive to wheat, for example, each time they eat wheat, they may feel better for a while. When they stop eating the wheat, there may be an initial period of feeling worse which is followed in time by feeling better. After avoiding the wheat for some time, a large portion of wheat may cause the symptoms to reoccur dramatically.

When one is unsure of one's food intolerances, it is possible to have a complex mixture of masking effects, withdrawal effects and re-introduction effects. The relationship of the symptoms to food will be far from clear. That is why it is important to follow a substitution/avoidance diet for six weeks.

My own clinical work with hundreds of patients suggests often that no changes are noted for at least four weeks. Many patients on their return visit have reported that if they had returned one or two weeks earlier, they would have said nothing happened or changed. However, they were happy they waited the full six weeks.

Some patients must carry on for even longer periods of time.

One nine-year-old girl who was experiencing enuresis (bed wetting) did not get relief for sixteen weeks. Then, after several weeks of no bed wetting, each re-introduction of cheese and milk caused a return of nightly enuresis. Needless to say, she decided that eating dairy products was not worth it.

Addiction or intolerance?

Patients with food sensitivities frequently behave as if they were addicted to foods. The sensitivity reaction may stop or decrease with a second feeding in the same way the cocaine addict's unpleasant withdrawal symptoms are alleviated by a snort of cocaine or an alcoholic's by another drink. As a result, many patients often crave foods which are the cause of their symptoms.

Food intolerances/irritants can have a significant effect on your health. I encourage you to investigate the possibility of food irritants as a cause of some of your health problems, to follow the recommendations, and prove it to yourself.

The chart on page ten shows the results of a study of one hundred people who had symptom changes after avoidance of their intolerant foods. While these symptoms represent just a short list of common complaints, you may also notice changes in these areas if you avoid your intolerances.

Common Symptoms Of Food Intolerance

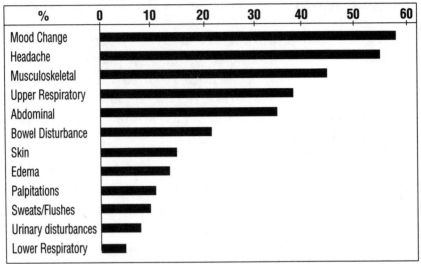

%	0	10	20	30	40	50	60

Mood Change
Headache
Musculoskeletal
Upper Respiratory
Abdominal
Bowel Disturbance
Skin
Edema
Palpitations
Sweats/Flushes
Urinary disturbances
Lower Respiratory

The chart above shows symptoms that improved in a group of one hundred people after they avoided foods that they were sensitive to.

Evaluating change

You should fill out the symptom checklist on page fifty-one and fifty-two before you start any dietary changes based on your food intolerances/irritants. After the avoidance period (commonly six weeks), you can then compare any changes which may have occurred by re-evaluating the form. I have often observed changes in patients without their realizing anything had changed, because the changes were so slow and gradual. As many symptoms began to appear over a long period of time, they may also disappear over a long period of time. In Chinese medicine there is a saying that for every year you have had a problem, it will take that many months to reverse the problem.

With food intolerances and irritants, it is important to remember that not only must the foods be eliminated, but emphasis must be placed on building health using therapies which can aid and support the immune system.

The triangle on the next page is a simplified representation of your health at any one time. Throughout our life we are

Some Determinants Of Health And Wellness

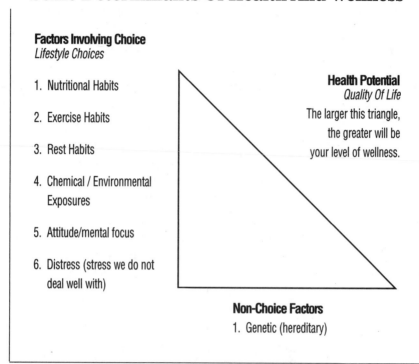

Factors Involving Choice
Lifestyle Choices

1. Nutritional Habits

2. Exercise Habits

3. Rest Habits

4. Chemical / Environmental
   Exposures

5. Attitude/mental focus

6. Distress (stress we do not
   deal well with)

Health Potential
Quality Of Life
The larger this triangle,
the greater will be
your level of wellness.

Non-Choice Factors
1. Genetic (hereditary)

Even though we can do nothing about some determinants of our health, we can improve our overall health by improving the factors on the vertical axis above.

continually striving to reach our health potential and maximize the quality of life. If you feel you are presently not at your health potential, then you need to evaluate the factors which may enhance your health.

Some major factors which affect your health potential or quality of life are listed on the left side of the triangle. Reaching your health potential involves many factors. We have no control over the genetic (hereditary) factors but we can (and do) make choices concerning many other factors. Health is not attained by luck (unless you chose your parents well).

Dr. Weston Price, author of *Nutrition and Physical Degeneration,* Price-Pottenger Foundation, 1945, San Diego, CA; republished 1989 by Keats Pub., New Canaan, CT, left his dental practice in the early 1920s to study primitive populations to find a theory for dental decay. The diet of Eskimos, Northern Canadian Indians, Masai in Africa, Swiss in isolated valleys, Natives on isolated islands in the North Sea, and Natives in New Guinea and Australia was free of processed food and sugar. Their diets were dependent on the environment where they lived. In addition to flawless teeth, Price also observed well-proportioned bodies, flawless skin, shining hair, clear eyes and pleasant dispositions. When foods of commerce were introduced into their diet, they lost their beauty and their health. It became obvious that the genetic potential of these people was also determined by their primitive diets. Whole food was the key to robust health and it affected the next generation.

Achieving your maximum health potential is a constant challenge in balancing all factors which affect you. It is important that you make the best choices about the foods you eat, the activity you do, how you interact with the environment, your mental attitude and how you have learned to handle stress.

Choice, not chance, will determine your destiny.

Diet changes can be creative, fun and uniquely rewarding or it can be painfully boring and relatively unproductive. The choice is yours.

Health potential

Throughout our lives, we are constantly hoping to achieve the highest level of health and wellness possible. The triangle on page eleven represents where you are at any particular time regarding your health. If you are not presently at the level of health you desire, then it means you are not at your health potential. If you can honestly say that there is nothing about yourself that you would like to be different, then I suggest you just keep doing what you are doing. (I have never met anyone who felt that they were at their optimum level of wellness but if you are, you have my sincere congratulations).

Health Improvement After Lifestyle Changes

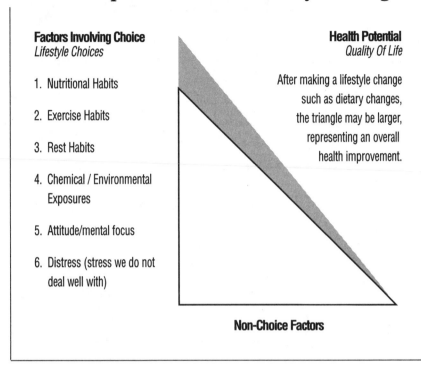

Factors Involving Choice
Lifestyle Choices

1. Nutritional Habits

2. Exercise Habits

3. Rest Habits

4. Chemical / Environmental
   Exposures

5. Attitude/mental focus

6. Distress (stress we do not
   deal well with)

Health Potential
Quality Of Life

After making a lifestyle change
such as dietary changes,
the triangle may be larger,
representing an overall
health improvement.

Non-Choice Factors

The total area of the triangle, representing overall health, increases as we improve the factors involving choice in our lifestyle.

What is your excuse?

Many people will have excuses as to why they cannot change some of the above factors. *Remember: the beliefs which have led you to where you are today are not the same as those which will lead you to where you wish to go.* If you are ready to make a change in your health, then now is the time is start.

Stress

Stress can come in many forms and something that stresses one person may have little effect on another person. The *perception* that something is stressful is more important than the objective stress itself. A few common stressors in our lives may include: abrupt diet changes, crowds of people, changing

Stressors, Health, And Disease

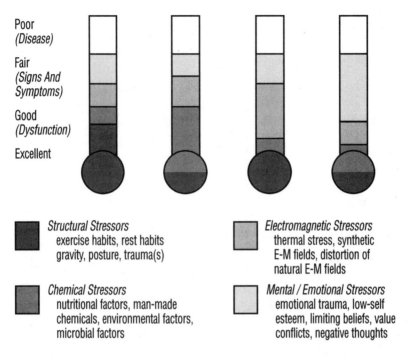

Poor
(Disease)

Fair
(Signs And
Symptoms)

Good
(Dysfunction)

Excellent

Structural Stressors
exercise habits, rest habits
gravity, posture, trauma(s)

Chemical Stressors
nutritional factors, man-made
chemicals, environmental factors,
microbial factors

Electromagnetic Stressors
thermal stress, synthetic
E-M fields, distortion of
natural E-M fields

Mental / Emotional Stressors
emotional trauma, low-self
esteem, limiting beliefs, value
conflicts, negative thoughts

Stressors of different types, added together, may result in poor health.

jobs, travel, irregularity, presence of strangers, fatigue, illness, temperature, abrupt weather changes, anxiety, bereavement, family arguments, broken homes, surgery, drugs, and crime. The nervous system and endocrine system are intimately involved in the response to stress and can alter nutritional processes and increase the needs of tissues for nutrients.

After making a change in any of the factors over which you have some control, you can expect a change in your health. If you make dietary changes based on removal, avoidance or substitution of irritant foods, you will be able to evaluate how much affect these foods are having on your health after about six weeks.

The expanded area on the graphic on page thirteen (compare to the graphic on page eleven) represents this change.

Tolerance Level And Health

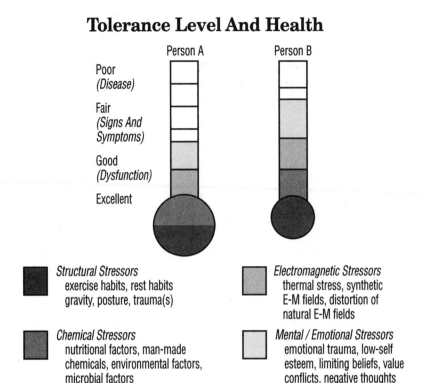

Person A has a bigger "thermometer" indicating better inherent health, and can tolerate greater stress than can Person B. Person B can improve their health by reducing stressors or by building stronger health through lifestyle changes.

Identifying key stressors

While this book is focused on the identification and treatment of food intolerances, it is important to note that there are many other reasons for health problems. Not all signs and symptoms are a result of nutritional problems. If you do not achieve the level of health you desire after following a nutritional plan for a definite period of time, review the "thermometer" charts above and on the facing page. They should help you identify other areas of your life and lifestyle that may need improvement before you reach your health potential.

These stressors affect all of us, but all to a different degree. This should help you realize that the same treatment will often not be equally successful in two patients with the same condition. For example people with constipation will often be prescribed a certain medicine. In some cases it will help, in others it will not. The reason should be obvious. With four patients, the cause of the problem may be different for each one. One patient may have a constipation problem because of a sedentary lifestyle, another from poor dietary habits, another from exposure to chronic damp, cold conditions and the fourth from emotional trauma. To properly address the condition, it is necessary to find the cause and then treat the problem. Treating signs and symptoms is not the solution for health optimization. How many people do you know that get headaches from an Advil or Tylenol deficiency? Treating the symptom is not the solution.

I am often reminded by some of my patients that they knew someone who lived to be a hundred, despite the fact that they drank alcohol and smoked a pack of cigarettes a day. They are invariably looking for justification for not making the necessary changes in their own lifestyle. The chart on page fifteen will show why a few people can "get away with it," while all the rest of us must work hard to achieve our potential.

Person A was fortunate in choosing his parents wisely and the enhanced inherited and acquired tolerance allows them to do things the rest of us cannot hope to do without some negative effects on our health.

The Food Intolerance Cycle

Cyclic food intolerance refers to food intolerance in which the implicated food can be tolerated when eaten infrequently after prolonged avoidance. Increased intake of the food increases the risk of sensitization. Typically these foods do not show up on either the RAST or skin prick test, often used by most allergists and other physicians for food sensitivity evaluation.

Read the diagram on the facing page starting at the nine o'clock position and reading clockwise. To understand the diagram it is important to review the definition of certain terms.

* **food addiction:** characterized by the dependence on a food; withdrawal symptoms arise if the food is not eaten.

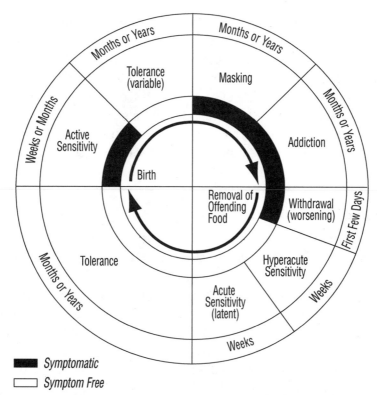

Symptomatic

Symptom Free

The Food Intolerance Cycle. Read the chart clockwise starting at the "nine-o'clock" position. An initial acute sensitivity may seem to disappear, only to re-emerge later as a masked or addictive sensitivity pattern. Symptoms may then get worse on withdrawal of the item, and sensitivity may become more acute for a while, but eventually tolerance for small or infrequent portions may be regained.

* **masking:** a condition characterized by chronic symptoms which resolve only when the person discontinues exposure to a food, chemical or drug which appeared to be well tolerated.

* **withdrawal:** the unpleasant group of symptoms associated with the removal of a food or chemical to which a person is addicted.

The "cyclic concept" is represented by the diagram. Initial *active sensitivity* symptoms which first appeared in infancy or early childhood such as vomiting, diarrhea, colic, asthma, ear aches, skin rashes, hyperactivity, or temporary failure to thrive are long forgotten. *Tolerance* seems to develop with the subsequent regular use of the offending food(s), although there are no evident symptoms. Avoidance and test exposures at this time may produce no evidence of a masked state. This tolerance stage can last indefinitely. In other cases the stage of *masked sensitivity* begins after months or years of regular use. The degree and rate of the progression seems to depend on the frequency of exposure of the questionable food.

Masked sensitivity state

Virtually all patients seeking food intolerance testing present in the masked state or the addicted state. Typically, an unmasked allergen is a food that is eaten infrequently and, when eaten, causes a definite symptom which can be detected without testing. With a *masked allergen,* on the other hand, a patient is totally unaware that the food is causing symptoms, or doubts the presence of a sensitivity. The implicated food is eaten more often than once every five days and most commonly more than once a day.

Many of my patients are often surprised that foods they have eaten for many years, often all their life, may be causing problems. The problem is often unmasked only after a period of substitution / avoidance.

Addiction

Food sensitivities may be *addictive.* Foodaholics consume an addictive food on repeated occasions to temporarily avoid withdrawal symptoms. They are on a continuous "maintenance dose," subconsciously acting to keep themselves symptom-free. By frequently eating the addictive substance, the individual can maintain an "up" feeling. Some foodaholics may never crave any particular food as they have arranged their eating habits so that the unrecognized, addictive food is always included in their meal.

A forty-seven year-old female presented to my office and said she just didn't feel well. Removing sugar from her diet resulted in a "new person" who commented that she now had her life back. After nine months of feeling quite well she decided to go all out and eat whatever she wanted. One day of eating a few chocolate chip cookies resulted in an upset, angry, irritable person. She realized it just wasn't worth it.

The phenomena of masking and addiction may be confusing because they involve an inversion of the expected response. Avoidance may result in the worsening of symptoms and the eating of the food will produce an initial improvement. This results in the paradox that a chronically occurring symptom could be associated with the ingestion of a food that tends to also make you feel better.

Hypersensitive state

In the weeks following the avoidance of the offending foods, the person seems to be in a hypersensitive state on the re-introduction of those foods. To understand this, compare your body before the removal of the foods to a muddy pond. Continuing to eat an offending food seems to make no change in the color of the pond. However, once you have avoided the foods for a period of six weeks, the body has cleaned out some toxins and the pond has "cleared." One exposure of the offending food can then cause a strong reaction, just as adding a bucket of mud to a clean pond could cause a noticeable change in color in the pond.

This state isn't necessarily permanent. In time, there will be some foods which a person can tolerate and other foods which possibly should be permanently avoided.

One of the most interesting aspects of this concept is that it was first described in 1944 and yet it is still not recognized by many in conventional medicine as important in the diagnosis of different health problems.

Homeostatic Situation

Here there is a balance between health-promoting and disease-promoting factors, and health is maintained.

Wellness vs. Illness

The "balance" diagrams above and on the following pages show the delicate balance between wellness and illness. Many people, especially younger people, often do not believe there is much need to put effort into maintenance of their health.

This "balance" (homeostatic situation) is a typical representation of the health of a person who doesn't realize the presence of underlying food sensitivities.

The food sensitivities result in a malfunction of the immune system which is different from that caused by typical allergies and is recognized as *immune system dysregulation.* This may explain why many food sensitivities remain undetected for many years.

Most often, I see patients under fourteen years old and over thirty years old. It may be possible that the immune system of children has not yet fully developed and therefore they may have

Impending Sensitivity Reaction

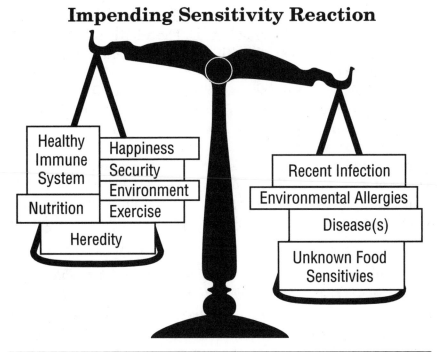

Here a recent infection has been added to the disease-promoting side of the balance, and the individual is more susceptible to stressors which might now produce overt symptoms.

repeated ear, throat or chest symptoms. Many parents are told that their children will grow out of their problems. I believe, however, that the food sensitivities simply become masked.

Immune system dysregulation

Immune system dysregulation can develop over a long period of time due to repeated infectious diseases, continuous stress and/or cumulative exposure to toxic chemicals — even at the low levels found in our everyday environment. It could also be triggered by a single serious viral infection, major stress, or massive chemical exposure.

The immune system dysregulation often remains undiagnosed because of the many seemingly unrelated symptoms. Thus, as you grow older and add more stresses, like your job, buying a house, supporting a family, rearing children etc., the balance again tips in favor of illness. The additional affect of an infection on the person's health may be to produce unpleasant symptoms of food sensitivity.

In time, say once a person is thirty to thirty-five years old, they may start to notice significant changes in their health. By this time, additional stresses have pushed them over the edge and illness may now become evident, although it will remain undiagnosed as an immune system dysregulation. As we age, we become more alkaline; most of us secrete less stomach acid after age fifty to sixty years which makes it difficult to properly digest our food. This may then lead to irritants from different foods.

Most of my patients will blame their health problems on some specific event. The conversation usually starts with one of the following: ever since I moved here, ever since we got the cat (or dog), ever since I got that new job, ever since we had a child, ever since I got a bad flu in the winter, ever since we renovated the house, ever since I was in a motor vehicle accident, ever since.... These events are simply the "straw that breaks the camel's back." Many patients struggle with their health after a specific event. It is time for them to address all the issues which are interfering with their path to optimal health.

In this situation, a typical ragweed-sensitive asthma patient may have no symptoms of food sensitivity until ragweed season. Then he gets asthma from the inhalation of the ragweed pollen, but also develops stomach problems from a milk sensitivity that may be dormant at other times of the year. Also, it may be noticed that if he avoids milk during the ragweed season, the asthma is less severe.

"This was the best hay fever season I have had in many years," report many patients who have been mindful of food irritants. The next patient to the office then says "This is the worst season of all time." Why the difference? One patient is

Allergic Overload Resulting in Disease

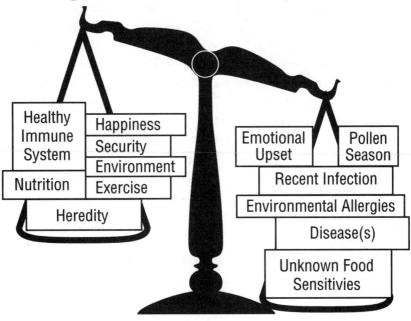

The individual, already weakened by a recent infection, is pushed over the edge by emotional stress and the onset of pollen season. The result is overt symptoms of sensitivity.

addressing the factors responsible for the balance to shift to the left while the other is more focused on covering up the symptoms on the right without making any attempt to "lighten the load."

What are you going to do for yourself?

Allergies and smoking

It is common knowledge that smoking is the number one preventable health hazard in the U.S. If you have allergies, intolerances or irritants affecting you, you're running an additional health risk if you smoke. Cigarettes pose four significant health threats: cancer, lung disease, nicotine addiction, and heart disease. But for people with allergies there is an additional problem of developing sensitivities to the various substances in the cigarettes. Nicotine, tars and flavorings create sensitivities, but in addition there is sugar. Every cigarette made in the US contains sugar which is used to cure the tobacco. So every time a person smokes, they expose themselves to a dose of sugar. The body does not take long to become accustomed to the habitual dosage and a sensitivity may develop. The intolerance, coupled with nicotine addiction, acts as a powerful stimulant that can keep you smoking every day. When you miss your regular dose of sugar and nicotine, you may experience an intense craving. The addition of the sugar makes quitting smoking even more difficult, but an absolute must if you wish to improve your health.

References

Hunter J, Alan Jones V, Workman E. *Food Intolerance* The Body Press. 1986.

Lessof MH, Wraith DG, Merrett TG, Buisseret PD. "Food allergy and intolerance in 100 patients — local and systemic effects." *Quart J Med* 1980;259-271.

Radcliffe MJ. "Clinical methods for diagnosis." *Clin Immunol Allergy.* 1982;2:205-220.

Chapter Two

Breast Feeding And Food Sensitivities

The best time to start feeding your baby right is several years before its birth!

Breast feeding is effective in decreasing food sensitivities and thankfully is making a comeback in popularity. The digestive system of newborns is still immature and the mechanisms for preventing food reactions have not been fully activated. Cow's milk formula has commonly been used to replace human breast milk.

Cow's milk

Cow's milk is low in iron, increases serum cholesterol (Oski), and is associated with insomnia (Kahn). It causes sensitivity reactions more frequently than any other food in infancy and early childhood. Nutritionally, it is very different from human milk. There is less vitamin A, C, and E, and much more K, B1, B12, and B6. There is much more sodium, potassium, calcium, chloride, magnesium, and zinc but less copper and available iron. The curds are large and hard to digest. The *New England Journal of Medicine* reminded us that dairy is not a basic human food essential for life. The American Dairy Council does not want us to realize or even know this.

Breast milk

Breast milk contains smaller curds and minimal amounts of foreign protein. Studies measuring the antibodies in the bloodstream of breast-fed infants were compared to those fed cow's milk formula. The studies suggested the inappropriateness of cow's milk in many infants' diets. Diarrhea, rashes, wheezing, colic, and vomiting were often associated with for-mula-fed babies. Mothers whose breast-fed babies have these problems need to exclude allergenic foods from their diets (Anon., *Nut Rev)*. This is often a major challenge to any new mother. Coping with a new baby is one thing, coping with a new diet can be difficult but it will prove to be rewarding. Mom may need some professional help to design a nutritionally adequate diet for herself and the growing baby.

What's in breast milk?

Breast milk has the appropriate essential fatty acids (EFAs) for the development of the brain. In addition to the vitamins, minerals, and essential fatty acids in the breast milk, there are a host of other factors which the breast milk supplies. These include immunoglobulins A, M, and G that kill pathogens (disease-causing microorganisms), anti-staph factor which kills staphylococci (bacteria), lactoferrin which binds iron and makes it unavailable for bacteria, interferon which reduces viral repli-cation, B12 binding protein which makes B12 unavailable for bacteria and lactoperoxidase which reduces streptococci (bacte-ria). This is partly the reason that in general, breast-fed babies have less diarrhea, less colic and fewer ear infections.

A seven-week-old baby was brought to the office because of severe colic and bloody diarrhea. The baby cried or nursed and slept for no longer than two hours at a time. Mom was extremely exhausted because of the lack of sleep in almost two months. Her pediatrician had recommended stopping breast feeding and using formula. Mom was determined not to give up and with a radical diet change was finally able to see changes in her son and she got adequate sleep.

Other reasons why you need to use breast milk

Besides the reasons already mentioned, other benefits include decreased obesity, malocclusion, finger sucking, and increased maternal bonding. Breast feeding will greatly en-hance the health of your children.

If you still are not convinced that breast feeding is essential for your baby, a study by Lucas et al. assessed the IQ in three hundred children who were born premature. More than seven years later, those who had been nursed in the early weeks of life had an 8.3 point higher adjusted IQ than formula-fed children.

Because allergies tend to run in families, breast feeding is particularly important for infants whose parents have allergies. The practice of giving cow's milk is undoubtedly contributing to the high incidence of milk sensitivity today. Failure by the mother to breast feed may be a common source of illness and disability in the later life of the child. The intestinal lining may be so severely damaged by milk consumption too early that the person will remain sensitive throughout his life (even though many people will think they have "outgrown" the sensitivity). Milk may also increase the sensitivity to all types of environ-mental allergies.

Not only may the child develop sensitivity to the milk, but (s)he may become sensitive to substances eaten by the cows and transmitted through the milk. Ragweed in cow feed may lead to hay-fever-like symptoms and bran in grains to a wheat sensitivity.

Common foods in mom's diet may be a problem

Breast-fed infants may have reactions to foods eaten by the mother and transmitted to the infant via the breast milk. Breast feeding mothers should avoid the common highly sensitizing foods such as milk, wheat, corn, tomatoes, nuts, chocolate, and alcoholic beverages. Many other foods such as eggs, oranges, apples, bananas, strawberries, onions, garlic, beef, pork, rice, soy, and coffee have also been responsible for problems.

Studies have shown that some totally breast-fed infants with eczema only improved after their mothers removed certain foods from their diets (Chandra et al; *Annals* 1979). Colic in infants has improved when mom stopped certain foods. Breast feeding mothers are still eating for two.

Newborns may react to a food the first time it is fed to them. The infant may become sensitive to a food which the mother ate during the pregnancy. It may be wise to avoid the use of dairy products during the pregnancy because of the high potential for sensitization of the baby. Mother must eat wisely, being sure to include whole grains, legumes, greens, fruits, and plentiful vegetables. Nutritional supplements should also be included. The mother should ensure the best quality and quantity of food to meet her needs.

Formula feeding

There will be some mothers who are unable to nurse their babies for a variety of different reasons or will not have enough milk to meet the baby's need. If you have exhausted all possibilities of meeting your baby's nutritional needs from breast feeding, then you must choose from the host of formulas which are available.

Commercially available products include:

*   milk based: SMA, Similac, Enfamil, Follow-Up formula, Good Start, Alimentum

*   soy based: Isomil, Nursoy, Prosobee, I-Soyalac (corn-free)

*   predigested protein: Nutramigen, Pregestimil

Homemade formulas

Formula #1

1 quart soy milk (heated to boiling and allowed to cool)
½ cup of the strained liquid from a mixture of blended
    mung bean, lentil, and alfalfa sprouts
1 cup organic carrot juice
4 Tbsp. maple syrup

½ tsp. chlorophyll liquid

1 tsp. flax seed oil

300 mg calcium/magnesium liquid

500 mg vitamin C powder

1 Tbsp. nutritional yeast

100 micrograms folic acid

Formula #2

1 quart soy milk (heated to boiling and allowed to cool)

1 cup organic carrot juice

¼ tsp. barley green

3 Tbsp. maple syrup

¼ tsp. nutritional yeast

1 Tbsp. canola oil

100 mg (or more) vitamin C powder

200 iu vitamin D

Formula #3

1 quart goat's milk

1-2 mg B complex (dissolve 50 mg tablet in 1 oz. dropper bottle and use 1 dropper each day)

200 micrograms folic acid

¼ tsp. flax seed oil

1 drop beta carotene (5000 iu)

1 drop vitamin E (25 iu)

Formula #4

1 cup brown rice

10 cups water

¼ tsp. sea salt

Wash rice and toast in a dry pan, stirring constantly until it is golden and begins to pop. Add to water and salt and cook for about two hours on a low flame, stirring occasionally. Squeeze out the cream with a cheesecloth. (This should be supplemented with breast milk).

Formula #5

1 medium carrot	2 medium potatoes
½ small beet	2 stalks celery
1 medium zucchini	3 large parsley stems
4 cups spring water	3 Tbsp. maple syrup
1 oz raw almonds	1 oz sesame seeds

Chop the carrot, potatoes, beet, celery, zucchini, and parsley and place in a large pot with the 4 cups of spring water. Cover and bring to a boil. Lower heat and simmer for 20-30 minutes. Strain vegetables out and add the maple syrup. Grind the almonds and sesame seeds in a blender and add the broth. Blend for 1-3 minutes until well liquefied. Strain through a fine cloth. Refrigerate immediately. Shake well and heat to body temperature before feeding.

This formula is recommended as an occasional or supplementary feeding to the breast feeding.

Some babies cannot seem to tolerate any formulas no matter what you try. One thirteen-month-old child came to my office with a history of "never being well." His mom reported a history of repeated ear infections, eye infections, bronchitis, asthma, and inability to sleep longer than three or four hours at a time. They had tried about ten or fifteen different formulas and all had produced undesirable effects. They were desperate to find something that could help their son. I instructed the mom to make the following formula which was made with products obtained from Thorne Research, Inc.

Dry Mix for formula:

1 jar Medipro (18 oz.)
45 Calcium Citramate caps (160 mg/cap)
5 Taurine caps (500 mg/cap)
9 L-Carnitine caps (330 mg/cap)
1 teaspoon Lite salt (sodium/potassium chloride)

Oil Mix for formula:

1 quart flaxseed oil (keep in refrigerator)
2 vitamin E caps (500 iu/cap of d-alpha tocopherol)
30 vitamin D caps (400 iu/cap)

Mix all wet ingredients together and keep refrigerated.

Mix 2 heaping tablespoons of the dry mix with 2 teaspoons of the oil mix and then add:

½ teaspoon acidophilus bifidus
½ teaspoon alfalfa leaf powder
1 pint filtered water
1 pint organic carrot juice
½-1 tablespoon of pure maple syrup (if necessary)

Within three days of starting this formula, the child slept his first full night. In the months that followed he had reduced infections, steadily gained weight, moods were dramatically better and his parents were able to resume a more normal life.

Introduction of solid foods

The purpose of digestion is to break foods into non-allergic simple sugars, amino acids and fatty acids. Babies are unable to do this efficiently until six months or so, and the notion that solids help them sleep the night is just a myth. They will sleep well when their digestive system is healthy.

Dr. L. F. Hill from the Committee on Nutrition of the American Academy of Pediatrics on the Feeding of Solid Foods to Infants, is quoted as saying "the early introduction of solid foods into the infant diet is the result of empiricism and competition, not of sound nutritional principles. It is attended by certain dangers, which are not compensated for by any discernible advantages." The more mature the infant's digestive system is at the time of introduction of solid foods, the more likely they will be able to tolerate them.

What happens when foods other than breast milk are introduced too early?

The introduction of solid foods, especially those which have been shown to create many food reactions, should be delayed as long as possible (Gerard). In a study of 288 infants at high risk of allergies (parents or siblings had a history of food allergies, asthma or hay fever), it was found that if their mother avoided cow's milk, eggs, fish and peanuts while breast feeding and the child was not given these foods in the first year, there were fewer incidents of food allergy and atopic dermatitis (eczema) than in children who did not follow these dietary suggestions (Sampson et al.)

Because the infant's small intestine has enhanced absorption characteristics (relative to an adult) and limited digestive capacity because of a lack of development of all the necessary digestive enzymes, there is enhanced uptake of incompletely digested proteins or antigens. The infant's immune system may then identify these proteins as potentially harmful and attempt to remove them via the formation of antibodies. This has been reported in such common childhood disorders as colic, abdominal bloating and gas, constipation, diarrhea, skin rashes, eczema, ear infections, mood swings, irritability and behavioral problems.

The later any food is introduced, the more mature will be the gastrointestinal system. Foods should be introduced in small amounts, one at a time. New foods should be given not more than once every four days. Give only a bite the first time, increasing the amount with each feeding if no adverse effects are observed.

First foods

Carrots, beets, squash, zucchini, and asparagus are vegetables which are generally well tolerated. Beans, spinach, and peas should not be given before twelve months of age. Tomato and corn should be withheld until twenty-four months.

Fruit

Raw fruit, other than very ripe bananas, should not be introduced before twelve months of age. Cooked fruits may be tried at nine months of age. Apples, peaches, berries, and citrus fruits should be the last fruits introduced. Pears, plums and apricots are felt to be among the least sensitizing and best tolerated. Please remember however that ever child is unique and any plan must be customized for that child.

Grains/cereals

Rice or oat cereals, mixed with water or breast milk, may be the best grain to start the infant on at about nine months of age. Wheat should not be given to an infant before twelve months of age. Use single foods, not mixtures.

Cereals should be cooked in water for three to four hours. There is some evidence that poorly cooked grains may be responsible for many of the sensitivities in adults to grains such as wheat, corn, rice and oats.

Slowly does it

Introduce one new food at a time, preferably one every fourth day while observing for any reactions such as sneezing, rash around the mouth, anus or urethra, a change in stool, or perhaps a change in personality. Non-sensitizing foods should be rotated every five days to minimize sensitization which may occur when the same foods are eaten once or twice daily for many consecutive days. The following includes some typical foods and their approximate time of introduction.

Six months

Hypoallergenic, pureed, mashed foods containing iron;
1-2 tablespoons per day (organic foods is always preferred)

carrots	asparagus
squash	broccoli
cauliflower	artichoke
yam	zucchini
sprouts (blended in water)	

Nine months

Foods high in zinc and good for the immune system; 2-4
tablespoons per day; cook all fruits

papaya	blueberries
nectarines	blackberries
prunes	cherries
banana (very ripe)	grapes
kiwi	plums
pears	apricots
rice cereal	oatmeal
sweet potato	beets

Twelve months

Foods high in zinc and bulk; 4-10 tablespoons per day

acorn squash	cabbage
tofu	chard
parsnips	avocado
rice	quinoa
raw goat's milk	egg yolk
string beans	split pea soup
peaches	apple sauce

Eighteen months

Foods high in B vitamins and calcium

tahini	kelp
eggplant	spinach
lamb	chicken (free-range)
rutabaga	beans
buckwheat	fish (white, not shellfish)
spelt (a grain)	teff (a grain)
rye	barley

Twenty-one months

Foods high in protein

egg	almond butter
turkey	walnuts
cashew butter	pineapple
sesame seed butter	brewer's yeast
oranges	

Two to three years

sunflower seeds	cottage cheese
peanut butter	soy
duck	lentils
tomato	wheat
corn	

Resist the temptation to give the baby table foods. While it may seem cute for the moment, the potential health problems that may arise will prove very disruptive for the child and yourself.

I would like to give a special thank-you to Dr. Lendon Smith for his review and comments on this chapter.

References

Annals of Allergy 1979(Feb);42(2):69-72.

Anonymous. "Dietary cow's milk protein is transferred to human milk." *Nut Rev* 1986;44(4):135.

Chandra RK et al. "Influence of maternal food antigenic avoidance during pregnancy and lactation on incidence of atopic eczema in infants." *Clin Allerg* 1986;16:563.

Gerard J. *Food Allergy: New Perspectives* CC Thomas. Springfield, IL. 1986.

Kahn A et al. "Insomnia and cow's milk allergy." *Pediatrics* 1985:880.

Lucas A et al. "Breast milk and subsequent intelligence quotient in children born preterm." *Lancet* 1992;339:261-264.

Oski FA. "Is bovine milk a health hazard?" *Pediatrics* 1985; 75 (suppl): 182

New England Journal of Medicine 1985:312(5):283.

Sampson H et al. 48th Annual meeting of the American Academy of Allergy and Immunology. Johns Hopkins Children's Center Baltimore, MD. 1992.

Chapter Three

Food Allergy, Intolerance / Irritant Evaluation

By definition, an allergy is an abnormal reaction to a generally harmless substance, occurring in a predisposed individual and caused by an antibody-antigen union.

Food allergy as defined by an allergist is "an adverse reaction to a food that stems from a reaction of the body's immune system." It is felt to affect about 1-2% of the population. Most people confuse the word allergy with any adverse effect from food. What most people experience with different foods is an inappropriate response to the ingestion of a food.

These reactions may be from food protein, starch or other food component, contaminant in the food (colorings, preservatives) or quite possibly some as yet unknown factor. Words commonly used include food hypersensitivity, food anaphylaxis, food idiosyncrasy, food intolerance, pharmacological reaction to food, metabolic reaction to food, and food sensitivity.

Mechanisms of food reactions

There are several known adverse or toxic reactions to the ingestion of certain foods specific to each individual. These can manifest themselves by mental, emotional and physical disturbances characterized by confusion, fatigue, irritability, headaches, mucous congestion and many other symptoms. These occur through different mechanisms which include:

* Classic antigen-antibody (IgE, IgG) reaction; (true allergy reaction)

* Hypoglycemic reaction, especially from sugars and wheat, (up to 80% of people with hypoglycemia may have food sensitivities)

ensitivity to chemical substances such as petrochemicals, fungicide and herbicide residues, drug and antibiotic residues, preservatives, colors, waxes, flavor enhancers, other additives such as sulfites or MSG

* Enzyme deficiency syndromes such as gluten in patients with celiac disease or lactose in lactose-intolerant patients

* Naturally occurring chemicals in foods such as tyramine in cheeses and red wine which are known to aggravate migraine headaches

* Excessive macromolecular substances entering the blood stream secondary to irritation and inflammation of the intestinal mucosal lining

* Some as yet unexplained mechanism (Mullin)

Immune system mediated allergy

Immune system mediated food allergy results from interactions between ingested antigens (foods), the digestive tract, histamine-containing mast cells and circulating basophils, and food-specific immunoglobulins E (IgE) and G (IgG). IgE (immediate) and IgG (delayed) are the most common mediators of food allergy.

In the immunological sense, there are four different types of reactions. These include:

Type I — immediate (less than one hour)

With this reaction, an antigen (Ag) binds to an IgE antibody (Ab) which is attached to a mast cell or a basophil (white blood cells circulating in your blood stream). This union results in the release of substances from the mast cell or basophil which often results in a typical allergic reaction: problems such as sinus congestion, hives, bronchiolar constriction, and gastro-intestinal (GI) upset.

Type II — cytotoxic reactions

With this type of reaction, there is a binding of either IgG or IgM to cell-bound antigen. This often results in the destruction of the cell.

Type III — immune complexes

Antigens bound to antibodies, circulating in your blood stream, become deposited in tissues and this results in tissue injury. This type of reaction seems to involve IgG and IgG immune complexes.

Type IV— cell activation

This reaction is mediated by T-lymphocytes (another type of white blood cell), and follows contact of allergen with a mucosal surface and results in a delayed inflammation by stimulating sensitized T-cells. This reaction does not involve antibodies. An example of this type of reaction is contact dermatitis, allergic colitis, and Crohn's disease.

In the strictest immunological sense, only 10-30% of these reactions involve elevation of IgE. Food allergy diagnosis may be made on the basis of a definite, immediate allergic reaction to a specific food, or a reaction which is suggestive of allergy, supported by a corresponding positive skin prick. In the absence of such evidence, the less specific diagnosis of food intolerance is preferable (Lessof).

Immediate allergy reactions

A food-allergic person is one who has adverse IgE-dependent reactions to specific foods. The diagnosis can be made on clinical grounds alone and distinguished from other causes of food intolerance if the symptoms: (1) are immediate in onset (within one hour); (2) recur on challenge testing; and (3) include, apart from GI disturbances, such features as lip swelling, itching, redness, anaphylactic shock (a hypersensitive condition where exposure to the antigen produces an attack, sometimes so severe to cause collapse and death), asthma or eczema.

Delayed allergy reactions

Delayed food allergy does not appear to involve IgE antibody but rather IgG and, less often, IgM and IgA antibodies. Symptoms are delayed from one hour to two to three days after consumption.

Which areas of the body are affected?

You may now realize that adverse reactions to food are numerous and are usually more complex than conventional medicine's definition of allergy as an elevation of antibodies. Any body system can be affected by these adverse reactions. Clinically, the digestive system, the immune system, the cardiovascular system and the nervous system are the most frequently affected. Common clinical dysfunctions include cramps, constipation, diarrhea, hemorrhoids, Crohn's disease, colitis, congestion, inflammation, fatigue, hyperactivity, anxiety and depression. The weakest link in an individual's system is often the first to show a sign of dysfunction.

A study by J. Egger et al. showed that migraine headaches in children can be produced by the introduction of allergic foods in the diet. The foods were many and were not limited to the tyramine-containing foods well known to provoke headaches.

Because of the delay in onset of symptoms it is often difficult to associate the use of food with sensitivity symptoms. In addition, because of other factors, the response may vary from exposure to exposure. Food intolerances are far more common than many people believe. By the definition of food allergies, many allergists believe that only a few people have food allergies. For them, there is a short list of foods which cause only a few possible symptoms that are easily predictable. Those foods include wheat, dairy, corn, soy, chocolate, nuts, peanuts, eggs, fish, and perhaps tomatoes.

Methods of diagnosing food sensitivity

There are several methods for aiding the diagnosis of foods to which people may adversely react. However, they all have advantages and disadvantages, and there is no simple, 100% reliable clinical test available for food allergy/sensitivity testing. Identifying the reactants that cause common symptoms is not easy because the reactions may be due to immune-mediated reactions (as related above), intestinal-enzyme deficiencies, toxins, infections, neurological/psychological reactions or an unknown mechanism.

The purpose of testing is to determine in a reliable and reproducible manner a patient's food sensitivities. A comprehensive health history and food diary is often helpful. There are two broad categories of applicable tests commonly used:

1. lab tests to measure immune complex formation

2. experimental clinical tests which challenge the patient with suspected allergens and then monitor any reaction(s).

The following is a brief description of the tests most commonly used to try and detect food sensitivities.

Radio Allergo Sorbent Test (RAST)

This in vitro test (meaning it is performed in a laboratory vs. directly on the patient) requires a patient's blood serum and measures specific IgE antibodies, such as corn IgE, soy IgE, etc. The assumption of this test is that a person without a food allergy will have little or no food specific antibodies in their blood.

However some problems with this test include:

1. Factors other than IgE are involved in food sensitivity.

2. It does not measure IgG antibodies.

3. If on immunosuppressant drugs, the patient may develop IgG which may mask IgE allergy.

4. The level of specific IgE required to say a person has an allergy is high.

Thus, there may be many false negatives with this test. The person may be allergic to corn but levels of IgE are not high enough to be recorded as an allergy, so the result is recorded as negative.

A number of studies have shown RAST is not valid for foods because of the false negatives. Thus, if a person thinks they are sensitive to a food and RAST doesn't show it, one can't say the food is OK for them to eat.

RAST is useful for inhalant and hive-type problems. The test is not influenced by antihistamines or steroids and the results take several days to weeks to receive. It is typically an expensive test.

Paper Radio Immuno Sorbent Test (PRIST)

This is a modified type of RAST but results seem similar.

Radio Allergo Sorbent Procedure (RASP)

This is a variant of RAST but is slightly more sensitive and appears to uncover more foods because it measures some IgG complexes in addition to IgE.

Enzyme Linked Serum Assay (ELISA)

This correlates well with RAST but is less expensive. ELISA IgG and ELISA IgG4 measure IgG and IgG4 respectively.

Enzyme Enhanced Lymphocyte Blastogenesis Assay/Advanced Cell Test (ELISA/ACT)

This test is said to give virtually no false-positives and less than .2% false negatives. It will measure delayed hypersensitivity reactions, requires a twelve hour fast and then a blood draw.

The test must be performed within seventy-two hours of drawing the blood, assuming sample is stored between 10-30° C in an all-plastic container.

If you are using steroids, they must be stopped four days before the test; aspirin and antihistamines must be stopped two days before the test. This test is also expensive.

Food Immune Complex Assay (FICA)

This in vitro test combines both IgE and IgG (the idea is to reduce false negatives) and measures delayed hypersensitivity responses. However, moderate levels of IgG don't say much about the clinical picture; that is, IgG levels are not indicative of food allergy. It does indicate the body has been exposed to a food even though the food clinically may not cause a problem. IgG is, however, significantly involved in respiratory tract allergies such as rhinitis, hypertrophy of tonsils/adenoids, chronic cough and asthma.

Cytotoxic Testing

This test does not work reliably. Like the tests above, it is an in vitro test. It is based on the theory that foods to which a patient is clinically sensitive will induce visible change (damage) when in contact with the patient's white blood cells (WBCs). The WBCs are mixed on a slide with an allergen (food) and observed for two hours. A positive reaction (0-4) is marked by changes in the WBC. Grade 1 is 10-20% destruction, grade 4 is 80-100% destruction.

The test is subjective and based on the technician's observation. There are a lot of positive and negative results, as the reproducibility is questionable between different technicians. This test is totally taboo in conventional allergy because it was tried for inhalant allergies but got very poor results. There are many false positives with this test (that is, many times there is no allergy but test says there is). It does detect something, as for over forty years it has been observed that food antigen induces changes in white blood cells, but it is not clear what the changes actually signify.

Sublingual Test

With this test, the antigen (food) is put under the patient's tongue and the patient's reactions are observed — wheezing, pallor, fainting, etc. The patient's subjective symptoms are recorded simultaneously. There are many false positive reactions. It is a cross between homeopathy and conventional allergy, using very small doses to try to induce a reaction. This test seems to produce the most inconsistent results. There are several negative studies including ones which showed fewer reactions to corn than distilled water and objective changes found in patients using distilled water.

Neutralization Therapy

This test involves both diagnosis and therapeutic aspects. Different concentrations of each antigen (food) are injected beneath the skin. The tester then observes whether there is a wheal/flare reaction (similar to what many people get when bitten by an insect such as a mosquito). The neutralization dose is the strongest dilution of antigen which does not produce a wheal/flare reaction. A study was done in an attempt to disprove this idea (Podell), but it was found that it does work.

Scratch/Prick Skin Testing

This is used by conventional allergists who scratch a small amount of food under the skin. If a red bump (wheal) appears, you may have an allergy. Even with a positive test, there is a 50% chance you won't react when you eat the food. There are many false positives and false negatives. It measures only IgE mediated reactions which cause the release of substances, especially histamine (hence the use of antihistamines for many allergic patients). The histamines cause vasodilation, an increased capillary permeability resulting in a wheal and flare reaction within fifteen minutes or so. With inhalants, skin testing gives good results but with food it gives very poor results. A clinically significant response cannot be diagnosed by the presence of a positive serological or skin prick test alone, nor can the diagnosis be invalidated by their absence. Even when the food allergy is of the immediate type, skin prick test and measurement of allergen-specific IgE may be negative (Brostoff and Challacombe). The test is painful and time-consuming and not useful in young children because they haven't built up enough antibodies to get a positive skin test. In addition, the test is influenced by drugs such as antihistamines and steroids.

Kinesiology

Used by many chiropractors, the food is placed on the patient and certain muscles are tested for strength and weakness. This test is inexpensive, fast, and gives immediate results. As yet, there are no "scientific studies," but it definitely does work for some people.

Elimination/Reintroduction

This is considered the "gold standard" for diagnosis. It involves an elimination or oligoantigenic (few foods which do not commonly cause sensitivity reactions) diet followed by reintroduction of foods one at a time until there is a return of a symptom. The food is then avoided again, re-introduced again and if the same symptom returns you can assume you have identified the sensitizing food. This must not be done if there is any reason to suspect an anaphylactic reaction. The test can become confusing when combinations of foods are the problem. Although it is time-consuming, it is effective when carried to completion.

D'Adamo Blood Type

Dr. James D'Adamo has developed diets and exercise programs for each of the four different blood types (O, A, B, AB). It is based on research that certain diseases are more common among one blood group over another and also based on his own clinical experience.

People with type O blood seem to do better if they consume flesh protein and do a lot of physical activity. People with Type A blood are primarily creative and do better with low energy food and light exercise such as yoga. They are suited to be vegetarians. Type B people are a balance between types O and A. They are both practical and mental and can eat from a balance of both the animal and vegetable kingdom with a mix of light exercise and more vigorous activity. Type AB are somewhere between type A and B but are often towards one type or the other and therefore some are best suited for type A diet/exercise and others are better suited towards type B characteristics.

For a complete discussion of this type of evaluation read Dr. D'Adamo's book, *The D'Adamo Diet* (D'Adamo).

Electro-Acupuncture According to Voll (EAV) Testing

In a controlled, comparative study performed by Julia Tsuei, M.D., F.A.C.O.G., between RAST, RASP, scratch, cytotoxic, food challenge and electro-acupuncture according to Voll (EAV) methods of allergy testing, EAV test results proved to be accurate and reproducible. There was a high degree of compatibility of the EAV with the other five tests, especially the food challenge test, which is considered to be the most sensitive of the currently available tests. The study demonstrated great sensitivity.

EAV is a non-invasive energetic evaluation of a patient using a galvanometer. It has been used in Europe for many years to determine the energy imbalances of the body. The original German electro-acupuncture technique was started in 1953 by Dr. Reinhold Voll. This complex, time-consuming procedure involves measuring hundreds of acupuncture points. In diagnosis with electro-acupuncture, a slight potential difference (voltage) is produced between a tip electrode held against an acupuncture point and a large surface electrode (hand electrode) held by the patient. The resultant resistance is then measured.

Every living cell in the human body or in living tissue oscillates in a specific frequency pattern, like the strings of an instrument. According to how these oscillations are tuned to each other, we speak of a healthy, functionally viable cell or a diseased cell.

The EAV test technique is founded on the theory of acupuncture. The course of the acupuncture channels plus the relevant acupuncture points provide the basic framework. EAV has shown that acupuncture points bear a direct relationship to a specific anatomical structure or physiological function of the body.

Because of the complexity of EAV, a second major system arose known as BFD (Bioelectronic Function Diagnosis and Therapy) which reduced some of the complexity of the EAV testing.

In 1978, Dr. Helmut Schimmel originated the third major system which is called the Vegetative Reflex Test (VRT). It is the culmination of thirty-five years of German electro-acupuncture development.

Vegetative Reflex Test is a so-called Bio-Energetic Regulatory technique (BER). BER records the bio-electric potential of a person and is capable of revealing functional or so-called energetic disorders. Thus VRT is a bioenergetic measurement technique (like BFD) similar to EAV and measures the skin resistance and electric potential on an acupuncture point.

With the Vegetative Reflex Test only a few points (versus hundreds with EAV, sixty for BFD) are used, as the system is based on measuring against special test ampoules rather than organ-linked acupuncture points themselves. The response of the person to the test ampoules results in a "yes or no" reading, as tested on one skin measurement point.

All German electro-acupuncture systems depend on subjective aspects such as the influence and experience of the doctor, because of the need to manually measure the acupuncture points.

In the 1990 *Journal of the Medical Department of the VEGA Grieshaber* (GmbH & Co), Dr. Schimmel reported that the Vegetative Reflex Test had spread rapidly around the world even though it is still not completely understood how effect comes about.

It is assumed that the Vegetative Reflex Test involves two processes:

1. a known electrical process of measuring skin resistance

2. an unknown energetic and physical process

This model does not claim to be complete or true; the method is still in an empirical observation phase. In Germany, the Grieshader Foundation with the affiliated Academy of Research and Continuing Education teaches the most up-to-date information about the Vegetative Reflex Test.

In the meantime, significant proof of the phenomenon of skin resistance changes was shown by a scientific study at Utrecht University, Utrecht, Netherlands (van Wjik).

Vegetative Reflex Testing is being used as an investigative tool to determine the presence of sensitivities to food, pollens, molds, environmental pollutants, chemicals, etc., without directly exposing the patient to the potential allergen. It produces immediate results in a simple pain-free way.

There is no test which can guaranteed to be 100% accurate, so a food diary and symptom chart may help identify any additional foods. In general, this food testing procedure is approximately 70% accurate (Lewith).

Summary

It is suggested that modern electronic instruments, although considered experimental at the moment, can be used to measure acupuncture points, and from these readings, judgments may be made related to tissue systems and bodily functions. A wide variety of food sensitivity tests are available. They encompass a broad range of accuracy, sensitivity, specificity, patient economics, risk factors, suitability and comfort.

Whatever clinical techniques are used in the diagnosis of food irritants, it is always necessary at some point to demonstrate a cause and effect relationship between food ingestion and the provocation of symptoms. The exclusion of the intolerant foods is the most effective form of diagnosis and management so an appropriate avoidance regime is essential (Brostoff and Challacombe). No matter which method is used, if offending foods are eliminated, the patient will feel better.

References

Brostoff J and Challacombe S. *Food Allergy and Intolerance* WB Saunders, 1989.

D'Adamo J. *The D'Adamo Diet* McGraw-Hill Ryerson, 1989.

Egger J et al. "Is migraine food allergy?" *Lancet* October 15, 1983.

Lessof MH. "Food Allergy and intolerance in 100 patients — local and systemic effects." *Quarterly Journal of Medicine* New Series 1980;XLIX(195):259-271.

Lewith GT, et al. *Allergy and Intolerance* Green Print. London. 1992.

Mullin G. "Food allergy and iritable bowel syndrome" *JAMA* 1991(April);265(13):1736.

Podell RN. "Food extract injection for food sensitivity—valid technique or black magic" *Postgrad Med* 1984;76(2):59.

Tseui J et al. "A food allergy study utilizing the EAV acupuncture technique." *Am J Acupuncture* 1984;12(2):105.

van Wjik R, Wiegant FAC. "Homeopathic remedies and pressure-indicated changes in the galvanic resistance of the skin." Department of Molecular Cell Biology. State University Utrecht, Research Unit for Complementary Medicine, Padualaan 8, 3584 CH Utrecht, Netherlands.

Chapter Four

Six-Week Substitution Program

I assume that, using one of the methods in the previous chapter, you are aware of your possible food intolerances. That is, unless you are following the elimination/re-introduction method. With this technique you will not yet have identified all the offending foods. You will need to follow the oligoantigenic diet for six weeks before the re-introduction process.

Based on my own clinical, anecdotal experience and unpublished studies, I have found six weeks is an optimum period of time to follow any recommended dietary changes.

On a weekly basis patients call me after they have made dietary changes for three to four weeks and are discouraged, frustrated and want to quit. This is definitely not the time to give up and try something else. Remember the Chinese saying that it takes one month for every year you have had a problem for some repair to happen. Six weeks is but a blink of the eye in relation to the rest of our life. Let the body have the opportunity to show you what it is capable of. Numerous patients have been forever grateful that they stuck it out.

In conventional allergy, the re-introduction of intolerant foods happens much earlier (usually just a few days). However, as I previously explained, I do not feel that the exact mechanisms of food reactions are completely understood. As a result, avoiding a single food for a short period of time and then eating it may not give you the same result as if you avoided all the foods for six weeks.

For the next six weeks you should avoid all forms of the foods which you are intolerant to. (You should also exclude any other food(s) which you have found bother you when you eat them, whether or not they were found to be an intolerance.)

There is a wide variety of symptoms that people experience as a result of food sensitivities. Before starting, complete the

Symptom Checklist

Assess your symptoms before and after your Six-Week Substitution Program to measure what progress you've made. Photocopy this checklist and measure your general state of health from time to time.

0. never have the symptom
1. rarely have the symptom
2. occasionally have the symptom, effect not severe
3. occasionally have symptom, effect is severe
4. frequently have it, effect is not severe
5. frequently have symptom, effect is severe

Head
___ headaches
___ faintness
___ dizziness
___ insomnia
___ drowsiness
___ other

Ears
___ itchy ears
___ ear aches, ear infections
___ drainage from ear
___ ringing in ears, hearing loss
___ fullness of ears
___ other

Eyes
___ watery or itchy
___ swollen, or sticky eyelids
___ dark circles under eyes
___ blurred vision
___ spots before eyes
___ other

Nose
___ stuffy nose, smell altered
___ sinus problems
___ hay fever
___ sneezing attacks
___ excessive mucous
___ other

Mouth & Throat
___ chronic coughing
___ frequently clearing throat
___ frequent sore throat
___ hoarseness
___ metallic taste
___ canker sores
___ dry or itching in mouth
___ other

Digestive Tract
___ nausea or vomiting
___ diarrhea
___ constipation
___ bloated feeling
___ belching or passing gas
___ stomach pains or cramps
___ heartburn
___ other

checklist above, using the point scale to rate any of your symptoms. Add any other symptoms you may experience which are not listed.

You will be able to use this information to help assess the

Joints & Muscles
___ pains or aches in joints
___ arthritis
___ stiffness
___ pains or aches in muscles
___ weakness
___ numbness
✓ swelling in hands or feet
___ other

Skin
___ acne
___ hives, rash, or dry skin
___ hair loss
✓ flushing or hot flashes
✓ excessive sweating
___ change in color
✓ dandruff
___ other

Heart
___ irregular heart beat
✓ rapid or pounding heart
___ chest pain
___ other

Lungs
___ chest congestion
___ asthma, bronchitis
___ shortness of breath
___ difficulty breathing

Energy & Activity
✓ restlessness
✓ fatigue, sluggishness
___ apathy, lethargy
___ hyperactivity

Weight
___ present weight _____ pounds
✓ binge eating/drinking
✓ water retention
✓ crave certain foods—which ones?

Mind
✓ poor memory
✓ poor comprehension
✓ poor concentration
___ poor physical coordination
___ difficulty making decisions
✓ stuttering
___ learning disabilities
___ other

Emotions
___ mood swings
___ anxiety, fears
___ nervousness
___ anger, irritability
___ aggressiveness
___ depression
___ other

Other
___ frequent illness
___ frequent/urgent urination
✓ genital itch or discharge

___ anything else?
___
___

changes and improvements in your health. By the end of six weeks, many people are able to evaluate how much change has occurred in their health by the positive substitution of other foods for their intolerances.

Earlier I spoke of the determinants of health. By altering any the factors discussed, you will be able to improve your quality of life by altering your health potential. For purposes of illustration, I have taken the straight line representing health, and made it into a circle. The circles on the chart below represent all the factors which influence your ability to achieve optimal health. These factors include both the ones over which you have a choice and those where choice is not an option.

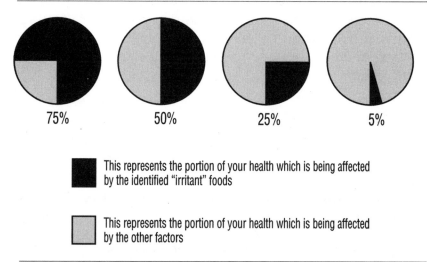

| 75% | 50% | 25% | 5% |

■ This represents the portion of your health which is being affected by the identified "irritant" foods

□ This represents the portion of your health which is being affected by the other factors

Different people are affected by foods to different extents. After a six-week elimination diet, you will should be able to identify what portion of your health problems have been due to food intolerance.

The darkened areas of the circles are representative of how much effect food and nutrition have on your overall health. The gray areas are representative of the other factors which affect you. These would include such things as your exercise level, environmental factors, mental/emotional factors, your job, your family, etc.

Each of us is unique. Just as our fingerprints are all different, so are our nutritional needs and tolerances. What may be an ideal choice of foods for one person may easily make another ill. Optimal nutritional health is a constant search for the ideal program which will help you achieve your maximum mental and physical peak.

After the six-week substitution program many people are disappointed that all their symptoms have not gone away. Please remember that there are many other factors which may be affecting you.

Some of my patients report little change in their health after avoiding the offending foods for six weeks. It is possible that the testing was inaccurate, or that the patient continued to eat their intolerances in "hidden" foods, or that for them, diet and nutrition are not the most important factors affecting their health. For these people, it is then important to continue the search for other areas which may be causing symptoms and problems.

They can't believe how good they feel

Patients who are dramatically affected by what they eat will often report feeling 75% or more better when they don't eat their intolerances. For these people, it is important to continue to fine tune their diet as they experience more improvement with further changes.

A fifty-three year-old female came to my office and described a forty-year history of bilateral wrist pain. She told me that she had been diagnosed at age thirteen with juvenile rheumatoid arthritis. Over the forty years she had tried every treatment known and estimated it had cost her tens of thousands of dollars to visit dozens of physicians and specialists only to achieve limited success. After the removal of wheat from her diet, she reported a complete disappearance of the wrist pain. Re-introduction of the wheat into her diet resulted in a return of the pain. She has decided she doesn't need to eat wheat anymore, despite the fact that it is extremely challenging.

Variety is key

It is important to remember that the main idea of avoiding food intolerances is not to further restrict one's choices of foods, but rather to increase the number of foods one eats. Most people typically choose the same foods over and over. In several surveys I have done, many people choose from fewer than thirty foods on a consistent basis. They shop every week or every other week and buy the same foods. By adding new foods, such as different fruits, different vegetables, different grains, different nuts and seeds, they will actually expand the number of foods that they commonly eat. I have then commonly observed that many patients will be able to tolerate most foods as long as a food is not eaten too frequently.

After six weeks, determine which circle most closely matches your personal health. Fill out the symptom checklist again to evaluate the changes which occurred.

Many times my patients will return and report that they don't believe anything changed with the dietary changes. That is, until they are reminded to fill out the symptom check list again. One middle aged women did not realize that her energy had improved. During our conversation she reported to me something she saw on the late news. I reminded her that on earlier visits, she had said she was in bed by 9:30 P.M. The change had been slow and subtle. The mind has a way of forgetting things when they are no longer apparent.

Why does it seem OK to sometimes eat any food?

Many patients have often asked me why it is that under some circumstances they can eat anything they want, sometimes they cannot seem to tolerate anything, and sometimes they eat a food and it is OK, only to be a problem the next day or next week.

I believe that your tolerance to the food changes with different factors that affect your immune system.

The following graphs depict the tolerance level changing

under differing circumstances. In high stress situations, it may take only a few foods to create a symptom. When some everyday stresses have been removed, such as being on vacation for some people, it will take many more exposures before a person has a symptom due to ingestion of foods.

The body's immune system is incredible. Its maintenance and defense mechanisms are second to none if you help and support them. Optimal nutrition, including choosing the right foods for you, can strengthen the immune system and result in a healthier life, a greater level of wellness.

I used to believe that most of the foods to which you are intolerant do not change very much with time. However, with continually increasing clinical experience and more scientific

Allergic Symptom Threshold
Under Normal Conditions

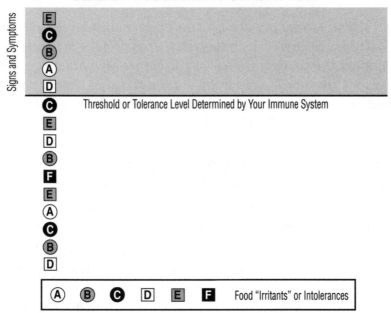

You might be able to eat many food irritants until the tolerance level is reached, represented by the horizontal line in the chart, where symptoms begin to appear. The threshhold is moveable, depending on the state of your immune system, the burden of food irritants, and your general health.

study, this does not appear to be the case. You may become intolerant to additional foods if you suddenly start eating large quantities of a food in an attempt to replace one or more of the foods to which you were found to be intolerant. At the same time, by using a wide variety of foods, it appears the body becomes much more tolerant.

The tolerance level does change depending on the other factors affecting your health. At times you will be able to tolerate the foods, at other times you will not.

I am often asked why people seem to have tolerated foods all their life only to develop "apparent" intolerances later in their life. It is very common for this to happen. The graph below shows what happens over a period of many years. If you

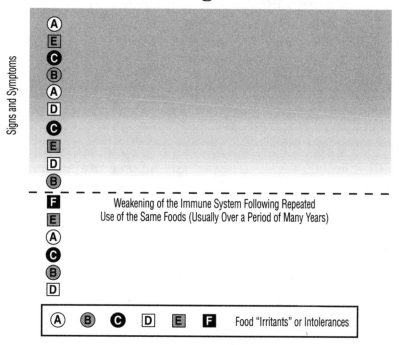

Lowered Allergic Threshold

Signs and Symptoms

Weakening of the Immune System Following Repeated
Use of the Same Foods (Usually Over a Period of Many Years)

Ⓐ Ⓑ Ⓒ Ⓓ Ⓔ Ⓕ   Food "Irritants" or Intolerances

Repeated use of irritant foods, or other contributing factors in the lifestyle, may result in a lowered threshold of tolerance. Good health habits, and avoidance of irritants, could result in a higher threshold, meaning that occasional consumption of food irritants may produce no symptoms at all.

continue to ingest a food irritant on a regular basis, I believe there is an eventual weakening of the immune system. In time (usually many years later), chronic symptoms develop as an attempt by the body to tell us that a dysfunction and imbalance has occurred. It is a signal for change. If we ignore these signals, more and more serious conditions will likely develop.

Food cravings

Food cravings are often an indication you are under high stress. Dr. Theron Randolph, M.D., stated that intolerances to craved foods produce a temporary improvement in the feeling of well-being. This elevation of mood is likely caused by an immune/endocrine system response. The temporary improvement is often followed later by an apparent withdrawal and a worsening of symptoms. This adaptation often makes you desire the very foods you should avoid. In some people this may be the explanation for compulsive or binge eating patterns. It is important that you especially avoid your intolerances at those times.

Many women crave chocolate during their premenstrual time and then report no cravings the rest of the month. After achieving a higher level of wellness, these same women report that their cravings have disappeared and they no longer could "kill" for a piece of chocolate premenstrually.

It should be obvious that it is important to learn to differentiate a food craving from genuine intuitive feedback and a strong desire for a particular food. Cravings are a result of conditioning and are impulses triggered by external cues, whereas intuitive feedback or instincts are a result of internal cues or tuning in to how we are really feeling. A food should leave you feeling comfortable and satisfied.

It should become evident that the true diagnosis of a health problem is much more than simply identification of a sign or symptom. Conventional management often involves trying to cover up the symptom without addressing the true cause. A typical example would be the treatment of heartburn with Mylanta, TUMS, Rolaids or some other medicine without identifying the true cause. I have never seen any patient who gets heartburn because of a deficiency in any of these products.

The true diagnosis of a problem, then, involves a thorough understanding of all the stressors which may cause a dysfunction. Management of food intolerances may control but one of the stressors involved.

Reference

Randolph T. "Specific adaptation." *Annals of Allergy* 40:5, May 1978

Chapter Five

Hidden Food Sources

The food industry has created a complicated system for most consumers. Many different words are used to describe common foods. **Read labels** as you modify your diet to remove the foods to which you are sensitive. The following is a list of *key words* to look for. The appendix section contains detailed lists of foods.

Dairy

If you are sensitive to dairy, check labels for:

milk	potassium caseinate
whey	calcium caseinate
dried milk solids	sodium caseinate
lactoalbumin	casein
curds	cheese
butter	margarine (some)
lactose	cream

Wheat

If you are sensitive to wheat, check labels for:

wheat	graham flour
flour	farina
wheat germ	semolina
wheat starch	bran (use corn/oat bran etc.)
durum	modified food starch
gluten	couscous

Soy

If you are sensitive to soy, check labels for:

soybean	tamari
soy flour	soya
soy protein	soy
soy oil/soybean oil	lecithin/soy lecithin
soy protein isolate	

vegetable protein (unless other source noted)
vegetable broth (unless other source noted)
hydrolyzed soy (or vegetable/plant) protein

Eggs

If you are sensitive to eggs, check labels for:

egg	egg white
albumin	ovomucoid
vitellin	ovovitellin
livetin	ovomucin

Sugar

If you are sensitive to sugar, check labels for:

sugar	sucrose
beet sugar	cane sugar
brown sugar	succinate

turbinado sugar (partially refined)

There are many other words used for sugar. You should also check labels for any of the following and depending on your sensitivities, you may be able to use one or more of them:

barley malt	date sugar
fructose (from fruit)	fructose (high fructose corn syrup)
honey	rice syrup
maple syrup	molasses

levulose (commercial name for fructose)
dextrose (commercial name for glucose, commonly from corn)

corn syrup (contains maltose, dextrin, dextrose and
    other polysaccharides)
invert sugar (equal parts of dextrose and levulose)
lactose (milk sugar, from whey and skim milk)
maltose (formed from starch)

Corn

If you are sensitive to corn, check labels for:

corn meal	corn grits
kernel corn	corn syrup
corn sugar	corn starch
corn oil	popcorn

Chapter Six

Grains

Grains have been a food staple throughout our world's history. For many nations, grains in some form represent the main dish at all meals. They are combined with supplemental foods such as legumes, vegetables, fruits, nuts, and seeds. They are nutritionally strong, providing high fiber, complex carbohydrates, minerals, B vitamins, low fat, and low salt.

A whole grain consists of the bran, germ, and endosperm. Refined grains have been stripped of the bran, and often of the germ as well.

The bran (the outermost part of the grain), has fiber, B vitamins, proteins, fats and minerals. The bran promotes removal of wastes from the body and also helps maintain even blood sugar levels.

The germ contains vitamins A, B, and E plus protein and fat. The endosperm is what remains after the grain has been milled and serves as a source of complex carbohydrates.

Many people fail to cook grains long enough. If your digestion is not strong enough to completely break down the many molecules in grains, you may experience gas and bloating. You may also fail to receive all the nutrients possible from the whole grains. The harder grains need more than an hour of cooking, preferably several hours of slow cooking.

Amaranth

This ancient Aztec grain has seeds about the size of millet. Its protein content is second only to quinoa because of the presence in quinoa of the amino acid lysine, which is absent in most grains. Amaranth flour is gluten-free. It can be cooked into a cereal or batter by adding 15-25% to another whole grain. It is also available in packaged cereals and graham crackers.

Barley

An ancient grain, it grinds into a very fine, white flour which can be used to make white gravies and to vary whole grain breads. While taking a relatively long time to cook, it has a tasty, nutty flavor and is a good source of niacin, thiamin and potassium. It may be used with wheat to make a light, yeast bread. It is high in malt and has a delightful, mild flavor.

Buckwheat

This seed is not actually one of the grains, (it is related to rhubarb), but because of its nutrient makeup is widely used in the same fashion as grains. As a result, it can be used as a substitute by persons who do not tolerate wheat. It has a fairly strong flavor, and, when used whole or as a flour, it is a good idea to mix it with one of the more bland grains such as corn, rice, or millet. It has a high biologic value, being rich in vitamins B and E and calcium. It deserves much greater popularity than its more popular use as buckwheat griddle cakes. Is available as pasta (Soba noodles) and without the hull (called kasha). Some Soba noodles contain wheat. If you are intolerant to wheat, please make sure to purchase those noodles which do not have any wheat.

Corn

Corn was first grown in North America, and continues to be the most widely used grain in this hemisphere. Being a large grain on a large ear, it grows luxuriantly and is an important seed crop. When used in rotation with the other grains, it is an important nutrient and is the only grain which contains vitamin A. It should not be used on a daily basis because of the high risk of developing an intolerance to it.

Corn can be used in the "milk stage" as whole kernel or creamed corn, and served as a vegetable. It has many uses such as in griddle cakes, waffles, mixed with soybean flour to make raised cornbread, chapatis, corn chips, enchiladas, and tortillas.

By using a coarse grind, grits are produced which can be used in a variety of ways: (1) as a breakfast porridge, (2) as a congealed porridge sliced and baked, (3) mixed with other grains, etc. Serving grits can be as varied as the imagination, the classic way in the South being as "grits and gravy." A variety of fruit sauces, numerous nut or soy spreads such as peanut butter or margarine, soyonnaise, soy sour cream, etc., are delicious with grits.

Kamut

Pronounced *kah-MOOT,* this ancient grain, believed to have originated in Egypt's Nile valley, has a rich flavor. While a relative of durum wheat, it is a member of the grass family and it is often tolerated by people with a wheat sensitivity (but not a gluten sensitivity). It contains much more protein and other nutrients than wheat. The whole grain should be soaked overnight and then can be made into casseroles, or included in soups. The flour can be used to replace traditional flours in any recipe. It makes excellent pasta and does not fall apart like some other non-wheat pastas. It is now available as whole grain kamut, kamut flour, kamut flakes, kamut bread and kamut snacks.

Millet

Millet is a cereal commonly used in Europe and is gaining much popularity in this hemisphere. It is one of the oldest of the ancient grains, dating back to 4000 B.C. It is often considered a weed and has been used mainly as birdseed.

Millet contains considerable protein, 11 grams in ½ cup of uncooked grain, as well as B vitamins, lecithin, and the minerals calcium, iron, magnesium, phosphorus, and potassium. It has a bland flavor and can be used in much the same way as corn or rice. It can be eaten by itself or with condiments, sauces, vegetables, and other foods. It is generally well-tolerated by people with grain sensitivities because it is easily digestible. Even though most recipes suggest up to forty-five minutes for cooking, try reducing that to twenty minutes to obtain a fluffy grain with a crunchy texture and nutty flavor.

Oats

This is one of our more common cereal grains of quite high biologic value. It can be used as the whole grain, can be cooked as a breakfast food, used to give body to casserole dishes and stews, and used to make patties or burgers. This important grain has many uses, and should not be thought of merely as "oatmeal."

Quinoa

Pronounced *KEEN-wah,* this grain-like fruit originates from the Andean Mountain regions of South America. Quinoa's origins are truly ancient.

It was one of the three staple foods, along with corn and potatoes, of the Inca civilization. Quinoa was then, and still is, respected as the mother grain.

Quinoa contains more protein than any other grain — an average of 16.2%, compared with 7.5% for rice, 9.9% for millet, and 14% for wheat. Some varieties of quinoa are over 20% protein.

Quinoa's protein is of an unusually high quality. It is a complete protein, with an essential amino acid balance close to ideal. It makes an excellent food to combine with and boost the protein value of other grains or legumes such as soy.

Quinoa is a rich and balanced source of vital nutrients. Besides its unique protein, quinoa also provides starch, sugars, oil (high in essential linoleic acid), fiber, minerals, and vitamins. While no single food can supply all life-sustaining nutrients, quinoa comes closer than any other food, be it from vegetable or animal sources.

Quinoa is light, tasty, easy to digest, and quick cooking. Quinoa flour is low in gluten and can be used as a substitute in baked goods such as pastries, cakes and pancakes with great results.

Quinoa's small, pale yellow seeds can be cooked and eaten in place of rice, couscous, bulgur, or other grains. The seeds are covered with a bitter-tasting resin that is easily rinsed off before cooking. The subtle, nutty taste makes it ideal for serving with vegetables, poultry or fish. It can be cooked ahead of time and used in salads, soups or stews.

Try using it in casseroles, healthy cookies, to make a high-protein bread or as pasta. See page 159 for some recipes using quinoa.

Rice

A staple food for more than half of the world's people, rice comes in long, medium, and short grain varieties. Rice produces more food per acre than any other grain. Brown rice has the indigestible husk removed, but still has the whole kernel and is rich in nutrients such as vitamins B and E, iron, protein, and linoleic acid. White rice has the husk, several outer layers and the germ removed and so is much less nutritious.

Rye

This hardy cereal grain is widely grown for its grain as well as its straw. Some of its species make a quick-growing pasture or lawn grass. The flour made from rye should be used to vary the nutritive content of breads, to make gravies, and to thicken soups and casserole dishes.

Spelt

This grain is related to wheat and is among the original, natural grains known to man. It was grown in Europe more than 9000 years ago. It is mentioned in the Old Testament and was last prominent in early medieval times. After the nineteenth century it was forgotten, partly because of its lower yield in comparison to wheat, and the need to mechanically dehull the grain before milling.

It is ecologically an ideal grain. It is not a hybrid like wheat and can be grown without fertilizers, pesticides and insecticides. Spelt can be grown in climates with difficult winters.

The spelt kernel is tightly surrounded by a very strong hull, which protects it against all types of pollutants in the air and also protects the grain during storage.

Spelt flour can be substituted in any recipe for wheat flour. Spelt contains more protein than wheat, as well as more fats, carbohydrates, vitamins, trace elements, and minerals. It is easily digestible and the nutrients are highly bio-available because of spelt's high water solubility. This permits rapid absorption by the body and often permits the use of less liquid in recipes. It can be used for baking, cooking, pasta, pancake mixes, and other uses, and is most often not a problem for patients with a wheat sensitivity. See page 171 for some spelt recipes.

Teff

This is an important cereal food of Ethiopia and the eastern African highlands. It is a leafy, quick-maturing plant which is well adapted to dry areas with a short rainy season. It has a protein content of 14% and is also a good source of calcium, iron, copper and zinc.

The grain is white or black depending on the variety and may be made into a flour and used as a substitute for other flours. The grain itself may be included, cooked or uncooked, in many different recipes.

Uncooked teff can be added to most baked goods or used as a substitute for seeds, nuts, or small grains. Because of its small size and high density, you use less teff than the substituted-for grain or seed. For example, ½ cup teff can be substituted for 1 cup of sesame seeds.

Cooked teff is gelatinous and adds body to puddings and pies. Its mild, slightly molasses-like sweetness makes teff easy to include in your favorite breads, biscuits, cookies, cakes, stir-fry dishes, casseroles, soups, stews and puddings. See page 189 for a list of teff recipes.

Triticale

This grain is a hybrid cereal derived from a cross between wheat and rye. In comparison to wheat, it has a higher protein content, with a slightly better balanced amino acid composition, and is more winter hardy. It makes a delicious hot cereal served with honey or maple syrup.

Wheat Flour Substitutes

Use the amounts indicated in the table to substitute for 1 cup of wheat flour in recipes. Note that many of these flours will not rise the way wheat flour does.

amaranth flour	1 cup
barley flour	½ cup
buckwheat flour	1 cup
cornstarch	½ cup + ½ cup rye, potato, or rice flour
kamut	1 cup
millet flour	1 cup
oat flour	1⅓ cups
potato flour	⅝ cup (good thickener)
quinoa flour	1 cup
rice flour	⅞ cup
rye flour	1¼ cups
soy flour	1⅓ cups
spelt flour	1 cup
tapioca flour	½ cup (sauces, glazes)

Wheat

There are many grains in this group of cereal grasses. Each of the different species has somewhat different amino acid content as well as vitamin and mineral spectrum. Generally, when bread is spoken of, one thinks of wheat bread. Like rice,

Cooking Times for Grains

Grain (1 cup dry)	Water	Cooking time	Yield
Amaranth	1½ cups	20-25 min	2 cups
Barley (whole)	3 cups	1¼ hours	3½ cups
Buckwheat (kasha)	2 cups	15 min	2½ cups
Cornmeal, coarse	4 cups	25 min	3 cups
Kamut flakes	2½ cups	20-30 min	4 cups
Millet	1 cup	20 min	1½ cups
Quinoa	2 cups	15-20 min	3 cups
Rice, brown	2 cups	1 hour	3 cups
Rice, wild	3 cups	1 hour+	4 cups
Spelt	2 cups	30 min	3 cups
Teff	3 cups	15-20 min	3 cups
Wheat, bulgar	2 cups	15-20 min	2½ cups
Wheat, cracked	2 cups	25 min	2 cups

Rinse grain in cold water and drain well. Bring water to a boil. Pour grain in slowly, stirring as you do. Let water come to a boil again, then turn heat to lowest possible temperature. Cook slowly without stirring until all the water is absorbed.

Many of these other grains can be substituted for wheat. In baking, the flours of these grains can be exchanged.

If you have cooked the grain the full time and it still seems hard or tough, add a little boiling water, cover, and continue cooking. Do not stir any more than absolutely necessary or it will be gummy.

it has been subjected to a great injustice in that the major nutritive properties are removed in the milling process for the production of a finer flour and a product that will keep for a long period on the grocery shelf. The long-keeping quality of white flour is due to the separation of the rich vitamin- and mineral-bearing oils which are likely to become rancid. Bugs do not so readily attack the white flour products, for the bugs instinctively recognize that the product is inferior and will not support their lives.

Wheat that has been broken into small pieces by coarse milling is called cracked wheat, while durum is used exclusively for pasta. Semolina is refined durum flour; couscous is made of either durum wheat or millet; and bulgur is cracked wheat that has been partially cooked and toasted.

It is very common to have sensitivity to this grain because of its over abundant use by our society. Even if you are not sensitive to wheat you should try to minimize its use and substitute any of the other grains. Especially try the less commonly used ones — amaranth, buckwheat, millet, spelt, quinoa and teff. Pages 197-208 contain a number of wheat-free recipes.

Chapter Seven

Milk and Dairy Alternatives

There are several alternatives to milk for those of you who think there is nothing else to add to cereal or use in baking. If you are not sensitive to soy, seeds, nuts, or rice you may choose one of the following.

Almond milk (Almond Mylk™)
Amazake (rice nectar) — Plain, Almond, Fruit
Cashew nut milk
Hazelnut milk
Rice milk (Rice Dream™, Pacific Rice Non Dairy Drink™)
Sesame milk
Soy milk (try different brands to suit your taste)
Sunflower seed milk
White Almond Beverage™

Nut and seed milks can be made quite simply in the blender. These milks can be used in any baking recipe that calls for milk. They can also be used in place of dairy milk when cooking a hot cereal such as oatmeal. Make only as much as you need for one day.

Soy Milk

Soy milk is available at health food stores, or you can mix soy milk powder with water. Experiment for thin or thicker milk. This is not suitable for babies who should be on breast milk or soy formula.

Different brands of soy milk have widely varying tastes. Do not base your experience of the taste of soy milk on only one brand. You need to try different kinds to suit your taste. One brand that many people like is West Soy Lite™.

Cashew Nut Milk

1 cup raw cashews   2½ cups water
1 tsp. honey (optional) ¼ tsp. vanilla (optional)

Blend dry nuts to form a meal. Gradually add water to form a milky consistency. Use less water if a cream is desired. Also try using juice instead of water if sweeteners are being avoided.

Coconut Milk

1 cup hot water   ⅓ cup desiccated shredded coconut

Blend. Strain if desired. If no blender is available, pour boiling water over coconut. Let stand one-half hour, squeeze out with a cheesecloth. Cool before use.

Almond, Hazelnut And Other Nut Milks

1 cup nuts   2½ cups water (less for cream)
1 Tbsp. maple syrup

Grind nuts in a blender until powdered. Add maple syrup and 1 cup of water. Blend until smooth. Add remaining water gradually and blend for additional 2 minutes. With a fine strainer or a piece of cheesecloth, strain milk into a jar with a lid for storage.

This will keep in refrigerator for 4 to 5 days. Use on cereals, in recipes or added to soups and sauces at the end of cooking. It can be used to make fruit smoothies and shakes.

White Almond Beverage™, Almond Mylk™

Commercially available, these nice-tasting products are a delight on cereals. This dairyless, soy-free

73

beverage contains almonds, brown rice syrup, barley malt powder, sea salt, carrageenan and natural flavor.

Sesame Milk

½ cup sesame seeds   1 Tbsp. honey or maple syrup
2 cups water   (optional)

Make the same as nut milks. Also try with juice instead of water if sweeteners are being avoided.

Sunflower Seed Milk

Same as above. Less water for cream.

Goat's Milk

If you are allowed goat's milk or are feeding it to a child, you must add 100 micrograms of folic acid to each quart of milk because goat's milk is deficient in this important nutrient.

Amazake

Available at health food stores, this drink is made from whole grain brown rice. There are several flavors available such as almond, apricot, mocha java and plain. To make this at home:

1 cup brown rice   4 cups water
1 cup sweet brown rice (koji)   pinch sea salt
1 cup warm water

Bring 1 cup brown rice to a boil in 4 cups of water. Turn heat down and simmer gently for an hour, or until the water has been absorbed. The rice should be soft. Let cool for 10-15 minutes.

Mix the koji and rice in a glass or ceramic bowl with the pinch of sea salt, and add the 1 cup of warm water to keep the mixture from sticking to the pan.

Cover the pot and incubate at body temperature (95° F) for 6-8 hours, either by leaving on a low electric plate or covered in a very low oven or even in a warm cupboard.

After it has incubated, the amazake should taste sweet. Bring to a boil (add a little more water if necessary but only to keep it from sticking). Boil for 5-10 minutes.

Let cool. Refrigerate in glass bowl or jar.

As a flavoring agent you may add almond extract, or perhaps blend in some fruit.

Magic Milk

If you can tolerate eggs (and don't have a cholesterol problem):

3 lightly poached eggs or 3 egg yolks

¼ cup water	½ cup oil
1 cup oil	¾ cup water

Liquify eggs and oil and add water gradually.

Pour into jug and make up to 2 pints by adding water.

Keeps the same time as milk in refrigerator, but whisk before use.

Excellent for a milk substitute in cooking.

Vegetarian Milk

3 cups water	3 Tbsp. short grain rice
4 Tbsp. barley malt *or*	1 tsp. malt syrup
8 cups water	

Enough ice cubes to bring 8 cups to 11 cups water
 (Add the ice cubes into a 2 cup measure, fill with
 water, repeating until 11 cups are reached)
 4½ oz (approximately ¾ cup) raw cashew nuts
 1½ oz banana (about ¼ cup)
 2 level tsp. stevia powder   2 tsp. sea salt
 12 drops vanilla   3 Tbsp. liquid lecithin
 6 Tbsp. canola oil

Combine 3 cups water, barley malt and short grain rice in a saucepan. Bring to a simmer over medium heat for 15 minutes. Cool. (If using malt syrup in place of barley malt flour, simmer rice in water for 15 minutes. Cool and then add malt syrup.)

Measure rice liquid and add water to make 3 cups. Set aside. In a large bowl, measure 8 cups water and add ice cubes to bring to a total of 11 cups.

In a blender combine rice liquid, cashew nuts, banana, vanilla, sea salt, stevia, oil and lecithin. Blend on high 3 minutes or until mixture is completely smooth. Pour nut mixture into bowl with ice water and stir well. Taste to see if you want to adjust the flavor. Ladle back into blender and blend, breaking up the ice cubes. Bottle and refrigerate. Repeat process until all has been bottled. Mixture will separate and cloud a little after you make it. Shake it up well the next day and it will stay emulsified for 2-3 days. This Vegetarian Milk will keep as fresh milk does and can be used in the same proportions in any recipe calling for milk.

Makes 3 quarts.

Dairy Substitutions

Instead of:	Consider:

Milk
- Almond Mylk™
- Amazake (rice milk nectar)
- nut milk (almond, cashew)
- Pacific Rice non dairy drink™
- Rice Dream™
- seed milk
- soy milk (variety)
- White Almond Beverage™

Ice Cream
- fresh fruit sorbets
- fresh or frozen fruit smoothies
- juice popsicles, juice ice cubes
- Tofutti™ products
- home-made "ice cream"
- Ice Bean™ (soy base)
- Rice Dream™

Mayonnaise
- tofu sour cream
- soy yogurt
- nut butter
- avocado

Cheese
- Soymage™ Cheese Alternative
- nutritional or brewer's yeast
- ground sunflower seeds
- tofu

Butter
- Blue Bonnet Diet™
- Diet Imperial™
- Fleischmann's Unsalted™
- Mazola Salt-Free™
- Parkay Light™
- Purity™
- Weight Watchers™

When a recipe calls for:	Substitute
1 cup milk	½ cup milk substitute + ½ cup water
	½ cup juice + ½ cup water
	1 cup water
1 cup milk (for baking)	1 cup water + 2 Tbsp. milk-free margarine
1 cup milk (for yeast dough)	1 cup ginger ale
1 cup buttermilk	½ cup milk substitute + ½ cup water + 1 Tbsp lemon juice

Dairy-free Sour Cream

½ cup cashews or Brazil nuts ⅓ cup boiling water
2 Tbsp. lemon juice 1 tsp. honey
½ tsp. grated lemon rind ¼ tsp. wheat-free tamari sauce

Place nuts in a blender and grind to a fine powder. Add the water and blend on high for 2 minutes, stopping once to scrape the bottom and sides of the container. Add the lemon juice, honey, rind and tamari. Blend briefly to mix. Chill before serving.

Yield ½ cup.

Egg Substitutes

1 whole egg =	2 Tbsp. liquid + 2 Tbsp. flour + ½ Tbsp. fat + ½ tsp. baking powder
or	1 Tbsp. ground flax or psyllium seed and 3 Tbsp. of water
or	Ener-G Foods Egg Replacer™ (contains potato flour)

For more than 200 dairy-free recipes, see *The Dairy-free Cookbook,* Jane Zukin, Prima Press, 1991.

Chapter Eight

Re-introduction Program

After six weeks, if you feel there has been little change in your health as a result of avoiding all the suspected food intolerances, you may choose to eat those foods at any time except when your tolerance is low such as when you are ill or under stress. (Note: I have had a few patients who while not seeming to respond to the avoidance of the basic foods or their combinations, responded well to the avoidance of multiple food combinations they were eating. If after avoiding your intolerances, you feel there may be additional combinations possible, it will be necessary to record in some detail what you are eating so that you may be able to figure out the problem.)

If there has been a significant improvement in your health over the six-week period, I suggest you seriously consider continuing to avoid those food irritants. As your level of health continues to improve over time, you may be able to tolerate some of the offending foods on "special occasions." These may include visits to restaurants, weddings, anniversaries, birthdays, and social evenings with friends.

If you have a definite improvement, say 25-50%, then you should choose one food you have not eaten for six weeks and eat a regular portion to test that food. (Note: if you have a history of ulcerative colitis, Crohn's disease or asthma, you must be extremely cautious on any re-introduction of food(s), because several of my patients experienced an acute attack.)

Once you have started to re-introduce foods, you may notice a return of past symptoms. The food should again be removed from the diet, the symptom allowed to disappear, and then try the food once again. The return of the symptom again will suggest your body does not wish to tolerate the food. Leave it alone for some time before trying it again.

One middle aged women experienced three days of vomiting following the re-introduction of yogurt. Her body reacted violently to a food it did not wish to tolerate. She hasn't eaten yogurt since.

In the following example I have chosen to introduce cheese on day one and day five. At the end of the week the important question then becomes, "How are you feeling?" Once you answer this honestly you will be able to decide whether you should continue to use this food on an occasional basis or rather leave it out and continue to use other substitute foods. The choice will always be yours. Remember that you will always be in control of what you chose to eat.

If you notice no return of any symptoms after the second exposure (day five) of the one food you re-introduced, you should be able to eat that food on a rotation basis of perhaps every fifth day.

Proceed with this same schedule for all the other foods you have been avoiding for the six weeks. You will likely notice that

Rechallenge: Reintroduction of Cheese After 6 Weeks of Avoidance

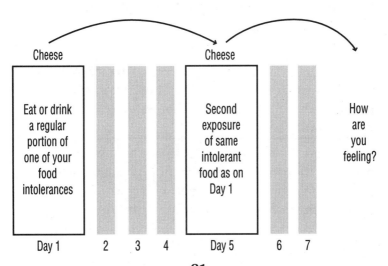

81

you will be able to tolerate most foods, as long as you don't eat them to frequently.

One of the keys to management of food irritants is the number of foods you eat on a regular basis. Since it is not uncommon to eat fewer than thirty foods, a key to a complete diet is a varied diet.

Repeatedly eating the same foods is not only monotonous, it may contribute to under-nutrition and the development of further intolerances. As you expand the number of foods you eat, it is also important to be aware of the vitality of the food. Try to eat foods in the form they are grown. For example, a raw apple is better than apple sauce or apple juice or apple pie. The more "life" in the food, the more it can help put "life" in you.

The optimal diet contains minimally processed foods. Factors which decrease food vitality include: transportation, storage, irradiation, heating, canning, dehydrating, freezing, thawing, and exposure to light and oxygen. Whatever you eat, always consider using foods with the most minimal processing and as close to its natural state as possible.

Principles of a rotation diet

Eating foods in rotation serves three main purposes.

1. It helps to identify specific food sensitivities. Since individual foods are eaten no more often than once every fifth day, each ingestion becomes an "unmasked" challenge.

2. It reduces the frequency of exposure of foods to which you are already sensitive. For those people with multiple intolerances, it produces a diet which is diversified and nutritionally adequate.

3. It reduces the risk of further sensitization to foods presently tolerated. Not infrequently, someone who substitutes one staple food for another eventually seems to develop a sensitivity to that food.

Rules for rotation diets

1. Do not eat any food more often than once every fifth day, even if you do not react to it.

2. If you react to many different foods, keep your meals simple, with only one to three foods.

3. Moderate servings are better than large servings for people who strongly react.

It is easier to begin rotation diet at birth because habits and patterns are not yet learned. Typically only the seriously ill are willing to make abrupt changes; in fact, they are usually willing to try anything.

Give it a try!

Most people need to ease into a rotation diet. As you begin, it is probable you will not be a one hundred percenter. However, don't disregard the entire idea of rotation if you are unable to do it completely. You may chose to start by rotating the foods in one family, say the fruit group.

This would mean that, for example, you may eat one or more of the following:

Day 1: peaches, cherries, pineapple, plums

Day 2: bananas, grapes, blueberries, cranberries

Day 3: apples, pears, papayas, mangoes

Day 4: oranges, lemons, tangerines, figs

When you are ready, you can add another group, say vegetables or proteins or milk substitutes. The variety will be good for health and pleasing to your palate as you learn to enjoy a much wider variety of foods.

Your whole family will benefit

It will be best for your entire family to be involved in the dietary changes. As your family improves their eating habits, you may notice that the so-called "healthy" family members remark about their increased energy and their improved state of mind as well as the disappearance of minor, but not insignificant, discomforts.

A twenty-seven year-old female had come to the office because of persistent headaches, sinus infections and fatigue. After her six-week substitution diet, she reported improvement in all areas, including her husband's moods. He had also followed the dietary recommendations and had lost eighteen pounds as well as decreasing his post-nasal drip which had caused him frequent sore throats. His support helped her with the necessary changes, but they both experienced positive changes.

I suggest using any food all day long and then not repeating it during the four-day cycle. It is not necessary to be concerned about a balanced diet on individual days, so long as whole, unprocessed foods are eaten over the four-day period. However, as much as possible each day should include protein, vegetables, whole grains and fruit.

The common goal of all rotation diets is to eat from a wide range of fresh, unprocessed foods. This will optimize your health while you are avoiding your sensitivities.

After avoiding a food for six weeks, you may notice a symptom on the first, second, third, or fourth day after re-exposure on day one. If that happens, you should again avoid this food. If you feel inclined, you may try to re-introduce this food again after another six-week avoidance. If you react again at this time, it will confirm a possible permanent sensitivity which should be followed carefully. As your health continues to improve with the other health enhancing ideas suggested by your Naturopathic physician, you will again be able to try the food.

If you notice a return of some symptom after the second exposure, say on day six or seven, then you should only eat this food a few times a month, say every eighth to tenth day.

You should continue this pattern of introducing a new food

each week until you have re-introduced all of your suspected sensitivities. (This may take several months depending on the number of sensitivities you may have.) During these weeks it is especially important that you keep a symptom diary so that in the future you may refer to any symptoms you may get from eating foods you can not tolerate.

This re-introduction program will enable you to determine which foods you should never eat, those you may eat every fifth day and those you may have a few times a month. This will enable you to plan for those occasions when you are invited out for dinner or when you go to a restaurant.

Some basic principles for eating

To reduce the chance of developing future sensitivities, I highly recommend the following basic principles for eating:

1. Never eat when tired or emotionally upset.

2. Create a relaxed atmosphere around eating.

3. Sit quietly, give thanks.

4. Masticate thoroughly, especially starchy foods. Put your fork down between mouthfuls and concentrate on chewing. Note the aroma of the food you are eating.

5. As much as possible eat "natural organic foods," avoiding over-processed foods.

6. Avoid eating certain foods too frequently.

7. Eat moderate amounts of food at each meal.

8. Do not overcook foods.

9. Avoid drinking alcohol while eating.

10. Do not drink with your meals, drink all liquids between meals. Drinking eight to ten glasses of chlorine-free water a day will decrease hunger because of the effect of over-hydration on the thirst-hunger center of the brain.

11) If you are still hungry after eating everything on your plate, wait five minutes before choosing more to eat.

The most important thing to remember when making dietary changes is that there is no such thing as failure, unless you put a time limit on your task.

Several patients have worked as long as a year before they achieved the benefits they were seeking. You can also achieve what you desire by continuing to work with the changes. Remembering the reasons why you wanted to make the changes in the first place will help you stay focused on the task at hand.

Chapter Nine

Allergies—Nothing To Sneeze At

While the focus of this book is on food sensitivities, I have included this chapter on environmental allergies. I have had many patients with typical hay fever-type allergies improve dramatically by avoiding their food sensitivities. The reason is because when you do not eat the foods which are weakening your immune system, it takes a greater exposure of dust, pollens, mold, etc., to reach your tolerance (threshold) level and thus react with symptoms.

Allergic rhinitis is known to most people as hay fever. Hay fever is just one of several different allergic responses of the body. Its typical symptoms include a runny nose, itchy eyes, sneezing and wheezing. Often the symptoms occur shortly after exposure to the offending substance. It is thus classified as an immediate hypersensitivity reaction.

In contrast, allergies to chemical substances, foods, and drugs may take several hours or even days and are referred to as delayed hypersensitivity responses.

It's not hay

In spite of the name, many people with hay fever are actually reacting to substances other than hay. The most common respiratory allergies are reactions to plant pollens, mold spores, house dust and animal dander.

Many of these offending substances — called allergens — are seasonal, and each season has its own particular type of allergen.

Different seasons

In the spring there are tree pollens, in mid-summer it's grass pollen and cottonwood, in late summer ragweed is common, and during the winter with windows closed, furnaces working, and pets in the house, allergens from mold or dander is a common problem.

Despite the year-round presence of allergies, most people only experience attacks when a particular brand of allergen is present. This is referred to as seasonal. Other allergens are always present. Reactions to mold or animal dander depend on whether the mold or animal is present, and is referred to as perennial.

Common allergens

You can acquire an allergy to almost any substance, whether natural or man-made. Any particle small enough to be carried through the air and inhaled is able to pass into the respiratory tract. This is why house dust, plant pollen, and mold spores are common allergens. Once the substance comes in contact with the sensitive tissues that line the nose, mouth, throat, and sinuses, the war between the body and microscopic invaders begins.

Defense system

The body's *immune defense system* has devised ways to handle these substances. Large proteins called *antibodies,* the chemical *histamine* and an army of white blood cells try to prevent the foreign substances from entering the blood stream.

For most people the war is a silent one. For allergic people, the smallest amount of allergen causes an all-out response. The swollen nasal passages, watery eyes and sneezing are all attempts to expel the particles.

When an allergen enters the respiratory system, it is immediately attacked by *immunoglobulins* (Ig), called antibodies. There are several types of antibodies, such as IgA, IgE, IgG, and IgM. IgG and IgM help fight bacteria and viruses while large particles like pollen grains cause production of the IgE.

When a pollen grain comes into contact with a sensitive respiratory membrane, IgE embedded in the surface of cells called mast cells, stick to the foreign substance. When the IgE sticks to the foreign protein (allergen), many events start to happen in an attempt to remove the invader.

The role of histamine

One of the first responses is the release of histamine from the mast cells. The histamine quickly opens the walls of the blood vessels and proteins leak out. This results in the typical swelling of the nasal tissues and eyes. This is the body's attempt to flush out the allergen.

Thus, to the misery of allergy sufferers, the body's attempt at helping you causes unpleasant reactions. In conventional medicine, the management of these symptoms is with the use of antihistamines to prevent or to minimize the histamine response, or commonly with the use of allergy shots. Allergy injections under the skin are done to promote the formation of IgG antibodies. These antibodies attempt to counterbalance the excessive levels of IgE antibodies being produced by the allergic person. IgG antibodies can block the allergic reaction from happening. Dr. Lendon Smith reported to me that in his experience with children with allergies, about 40% got better, 40% got worse, and 20% had no change in their symptoms after the use of allergy injections.

I have been seeing an increasing number of patients with auto-immune diseases — rheumatoid arthritis, lupus, multiple sclerosis, ulcerative colitis, Crohn's disease, etc., who have a history of allergy shots when they were younger. An overload on the immune system may be predisposing these people to an over-activity of their immune system later in life.

Natural management

I believe the best way to manage allergy symptoms is to maximize your immune system via a healthy lifestyle. This includes proper nutrition and avoidance of your intolerances, exercise, stress management, proper rest and relaxation and an enjoyment of life. This can do more to help you control your hay fever reaction than any particular medication you may try. There are many ways to help your hay fever symptoms. You should start building your immune system several months before your seasonal allergy flares up. Therapies such as nutritional supplements, botanical tinctures and teas, homeopathic medications, hydrotherapy, stress management, exercise, and lifestyle counselling are but a few avenues open to you. They can enhance your immune system and thus reduce or minimize your hay fever symptoms. For your particular situation you should consult a Naturopathic physician who can help you determine which therapeutic modalities would be the most helpful for you. You can be in control of your health and not at the mercy of the pollens or other environmental factors around you.

The appendix sections contain many tips to help you control the most common exposures of dust, mold, pollens, etc.

Chapter Ten
What Else Can You Do?

Dietary changes are very challenging, to say the least. You are not alone as you go through this process and it is important to remember that the purpose of identifying intolerant foods is to improve your total health. It is not intended to cause a feeling of deprivation or fear or to have you follow a severely restricted diet for the rest of your life. If you approach this program with a "have to" attitude, you'll probably not finish it. But if you approach it with the idea that you're going to regain lost health, your enthusiasm and motivation will sustain you until you see measurable results. At that time you will realize that you feel so much better, the changes will become a lifetime commitment.

Other healthful ideas

It is important to remember that dietary changes are only part of the help you can receive in improving your health. The stronger your immune system, the more you will be able to tolerate your sensitivities. There are many ways to improve your immune system. Several approaches to consider are discussed on the following pages.

Attitude

Develop a positive, productive attitude towards life. Seek a sense of responsibility and purpose and seek socially enjoyable activities for yourself.

Stress

Learn stress-management techniques that are specific for you to help reduce your stress level.

Chemicals

Minimize your exposure to toxic chemicals in the air, foods, and water. A study published in 1993 (Smith) compared the difference between the nutritional value of organic foods and that of commercial foods. The study revealed that the average elemental concentration in organic foods on a fresh weight basis was found to be about twice that of commercial foods. This suggests that buying organic produce not only will reduce your exposure to potentially harmful chemicals, but your produce will have a much greater nutritional value. The 1988 Surgeon General's report on nutrition stated that nutrition plays an important role in the prevention of diseases such as heart disease, stroke, cancer, and diabetes. In addition, Dr. Melvyn Werbach, in his book *Nutritional Influences on Illness,* 1993, cites study after study which relate how low levels of different elements correlate with many health problems. Supplementation of these elements then resulted in a reduction of symptoms. Your choice of chemical-free foods is very important for your health.

Air quality

The quality of air in most people's homes is many times more toxic than that outside their homes, even in urban and inner-city settings. Studies have found air contamination levels to be as much as seventy times higher indoors than outdoors. To create a superior environment in your home begin with the use of non-toxic, biodegradable household cleaning products, non-toxic paints, superior vacuum and air filtration systems, cleaner heat sources, and abstinence from polluting habits such as smoking and the use of any kind of chemical indoors.

Live, eat, and work in the cleanest environment possible.

Light

We need daily exposure to natural sunlight and should use full spectrum light. Conventional fluorescent lights are a stress for our immune system.

Water

Drink a minimum of six to eight glasses of non-chlorinated, filtered water daily. If necessary, buy a water filter for your home to ensure an adequate supply of clean, unadulterated water. Drink the water first thing in the morning, fifteen to thirty minutes before meals and every other opportunity you have away from meals, never with your meals.

Immune system stimulation techniques

The healing process from immune system dysregulation is often long, slow, and frustrating during short-term setbacks. The healing process seems to follow a roller coaster pattern.

If you haven't achieved the level of health you desire after the six-week substitution period, consider some of the following in consultation with your holistically trained Naturopathic physician.

1. nutritional supplements

2. homeopathy

3. botanical medicine (teas, tinctures, capsules)

4. acupuncture

5. stress reduction/meditation

6. massage

7. hydrotherapy (the use of water)

8. movement (exercise)

The ideal exercise for you must be fun to do and easy to practice. It will stimulate your inner biological functions with no side effects and make you feel energized for having done it. Many people start with walking.

9. physical therapy

10. *Anything else* which is determined to be appropriate for your specific condition. It is sometimes necessary to use these therapies during the avoidance period.

Rebuilding the immune system and regaining tolerance to foods is a gradual process and may take months or years. It will be important for you to continue to practice the healthful lifestyle choices which have been prescribed for you.

Naturopathic physicians are well trained to help you in any of these areas. Contact the American Association of Naturopathic Physicians in Seattle, WA for a list of the closest naturopaths to your home. Their address is 2366 Eastlake Avenue East, Suite 322, Seattle, WA, 98102, (206) 323-7610, Fax (206) 323-7612.

While avoidance of foods you are sensitive to is extremely important, it is also necessary to include "healing" foods. Naturopathic medicine considers the liver an extremely important organ that is involved in many disease states, particularly those involving sensitivities. The following foods may be especially advantageous in helping the liver heal. They should be included regularly in your diet and eaten as fresh as possible. Of course, do not include any of the foods you may be intolerant to.

apples, apple juice (fresh)	orange juice (fresh)
artichokes	green peppers
beet leaves, juice (fresh)	plums
carrots, carrot juice (fresh)	pomegranate
cauliflower	quince
cherries	radish juice (fresh)
collards	raspberries
cranberries	sesame seeds
dandelion greens, tea	spinach
endives	strawberries
gooseberries	tangerines
garlic	tomatoes
grapefruit	turnip greens
grapes, grape juice (fresh)	walnuts
lemons, lemon juice (fresh)	watercress
olives, olive oil	

Are you better or worse?

After recovery has begun, you may begin to notice adverse reactions to substances that previously caused no problems. This is the "unmasking" which allows underlying sensitivities to become temporarily more acute. This is to be expected. Although this is often perceived as a increase of symptoms or severity of the disease, it is, in fact, a sign of improvement.

During this period you may experience the withdrawal from previously unrecognized addictions. After having abstained for long periods, a formerly addicted person will usually have immediate and severe symptoms upon re-exposure to the addicting substance.

As your health improves you will find the frequency, duration, and severity of any "setbacks" gradually diminish until symptoms are mild and occur only occasionally.

But it costs to much!

I am often told that healthy food is too expensive. Health does not cost, it pays. Studies have shown that if you spend wisely, consumers could reduce their annual food budget. Use the following suggestions:

• Eat out less often; it is twice as expensive to eat out as healthful cooking at home. Bring your lunch to work or school.

• When you do eat out, make wise choices with less expensive items.

• Buy fewer packaged foods.

• Buy less meat.

• Buy more beans, whole grains, vegetables and fruit.

• Store food properly so it doesn't spoil.

• Don't waste money on junk foods, such as soda pop, hot dogs, coffee, candy, potato chips, etc.

• Grow some of your food in your own organic garden.

• Use sprouting regularly.

• Search out health food stores in your city which carry alternative foods. Food co-operatives are available almost everywhere and can represent significant savings when foods are ordered in bulk amounts.

The New England Journal of Medicine reported in its July 29, 1993, issue that people who reported good health habits (such as eating a healthy diet, engaging in regular exercise, and not smoking) had average health insurance claims of $190.00 per year. Those with poor habits had claims averaging $1,550.00 per year. Prevention doesn't cost, it pays.

The appendix sections of this book contains many ideas for you and I encourage you to look them over carefully.

Congratulations on searching for ways to improve your health.

Reference

Smith, Bob. "Organic foods vs supermarket foods: element levels." *J of Applied Nut* (1993)45:1.

Appendix One

Caffeine

Caffeine is a drug with primarily stimulating effects. It is found in foods, beverages, and medicines, and occurs naturally in plant products such as coffee, tea, cocoa beans, guarana root and kola nuts. Caffeine is rapidly absorbed from the intestine and within a few minutes enters all organs and tissues. The effect remains for about three hours and it almost completely disappears from the body overnight.

Caffeine has the following effects on the body:

1. stimulates the brain and promotes wakefulness

2. stimulates the heart

3. relaxes smooth muscle, the type of muscle in the digestive tract and blood vessels

4. increases the flow of urine

5. stimulates the secretion of stomach acid

6. increases muscle strength

Common symptoms of caffeine use include:

nervousness	restlessness
anxiety	irritability
excitement	trembling
headache	gastro-intestinal irritation
diarrhea	rapid heart beat
increased breathing	ringing in the ears
desire to urinate	insomnia

Caffeine is probably the most common food that patients have given up because of the undesirable symptoms it produces for them.

Caffeine Content In Foods And Drugs

Item	Amount (oz)	Caffeine (mg)
Coffee		
Chock Full O' Nuts (drip)	6	105
Shop Rite (drip)	6	101
Savarin (drip)	6	98
Perfect Balance (drip)	6	72
Folgers Instant	6	64
Shop Rite Instant	6	63
Melitta Extra Fine (drip)	6	61
Perfect Balance Instant	6	39
Maxwell House Instant	6	23
decaffeinated coffee	6	2-5
Tea		
Salada	6	49
Bigelow English Teatime	6	47
Lipton	6	46
Boston's Darjeeling Blend	6	38
Tetley	6	38
Salada (caffeine-reduced)	6	22
Tetley (decaffeinated)	6	6
Lipton (decaffeinated)	6	5
Celestial Seasonings (caffeine-free)	6	0
Soft Drinks		
Mountain Dew	12	57
Dr. Pepper	12	51
Diet Coke	12	46
TAB	12	45
Pepsi-Cola	12	36
RC Cola	12	35
Coca-Cola Classic	12	34
Diet Rite Cola	12	0
Diet Sprite	12	0

Chocolate

Milk chocolate	1	15
Semisweet chocolate	1	13
Chocolate milk	8	8
Chocolate-flavored syrup	1	5
Cocoa (beverage)	5	4

Other

alertness tabs	tablet	100-200
pain relievers	tablet	32-65
cold allergy relief remedies	tablet	15-32

(source: Rodale's *Food & Nutrition Letter,* Oct. 1991 Vol. 5 No. 10)

Health concerns

In amounts typically consumed, caffeine acts as a drug. Many people develop a dependence on it. When the caffeine is withdrawn, it may cause withdrawal symptoms—headaches, irritability, restlessness, and fatigue are common.

Caffeine is now implicated in many different health problems. These include:

1. It stimulates acid secretion in the stomach. Two cups may increase stomach acid for more than one hour. This may aggravate an existing ulcer, promote an ulcer or interfere with healing. This is especially a problem in patients with heartburn and perhaps one of the reasons for our antacid-popping society.

2. It has been implicated in cancer. While it has not been shown to directly cause cancer, it has been shown to interfere with repair of chromosomes in cells. Further research should help disclose its relationship to bladder and pancreas cancer.

3. It crosses the placenta. In animal studies it has been implicated in birth defects. It should not be used during pregnancy.

4. It raises blood pressure in sensitive people.

5. It increases blood coagulation. It may thus increase the risk of coronary thrombosis.

6. It increases mental speed (arithmetic, typing) but impairs motor co-ordination (target shooting, writing, driving). The improvement in mental efficiency fell off below normal from one to three hours after coffee intake.

7. It increases blood sugar and aggravates hypoglycemia and diabetes.

8. It increases the consumption of alcohol. In animal experiments, when coffee was added to the diet, the animals voluntarily drank two to four times more alcohol than the amount consumed without coffee.

There are many hot beverages available for people desiring a substitute for coffee. It is in your best interest to search for the ones which most suit your palate. Try one or more of the following: Roma, Cafix, Caffree, Inka, Roastaroma. You will do a great deal for your health by stopping caffeine consumption.

Withdrawal

Many people have experienced headaches when they quit or reduced the consumption of caffeine products. I have used the following protocol with success to help minimize the withdrawal headache.

- vitamin B12   1000 mcg. 2 times a day
- vitamin B complex   50 mg 2 times a day
- lecithin   2400 mg 3 times a day
- vitamin E   400 iu 2 times a day
- chamomile tea   4-6 cups a day
- use ginger, cayenne, peppermint in your regular diet
- 8-10 glasses of chlorine-free water
- regular daily exercise (walking works well)

Appendix Two

Calcium, Non-Dairy Sources

Most Americans are aware of the condition called osteoporosis which seems to afflict the bones of older people. This bone wasting condition affects an estimated twenty million women and five million men. Advertising has convinced many that they must use dairy products to help minimize this risk. It is interesting to note that the U.S. has one of the highest consumptions of dairy products in the world, yet also has one of the highest rates of osteoporosis. Countries with a much lower dairy intake also have much lower rates of osteoporosis. Don't think that drinking milk and eating cheese and yogurt will offer you the protection that the American Dairy council would like you to believe.

RDA for calcium

The current recommended daily allowance (RDA) is 800 mg; 1200 mg for pregnant or lactating women. It has been suggested that this may be too low and perhaps 1,000 milligrams for adults and even more for older children, young adults and postmenopausal women would be preferred.

It has become obvious that the need for more calcium starts earlier in life to ensure maximum bone density between the ages of thirty to thirty-five years old. Bone building occurs almost entirely during childhood and adolescence. By age twenty, the bones are about as strong as they will ever be and after thirty they stop growing and start slowly losing minerals that give them their strength. After menopause the rate of loss accelerates. By age sixty-five both men and women are losing bone at the same rate. Fewer men than women have problems with this condition because they have a greater bone mass to lose from.

The teen years are critical

The need for calcium is greatest between the ages nine and eighteen, when children lay down up to 37% of their total adult bone mass. Unfortunately these are also the ages when many children increase their consumption of calcium-poor foods — soda pop, fast foods, which prevents them from obtaining even the minimum RDA amounts of calcium. In addition, excess use of sodium and protein in the diet further deplete the body's calcium supply by increasing the amount of calcium excreted in the urine. This is just another reason for a low-fat, low-protein diet.

A low-protein and low-sodium diet may reduce the calcium requirement considerably. If you add a good variety of the foods listed below, you will likely be helping yourself reduce some of the potential devastating effects of osteoporosis later in your life.

The typical American's diet relies on dairy products for 70% of its calcium intake. One cup (8 ounces) of cow's milk contains approximately 300 mg of calcium. Eight ounces of breast milk contains about 80 mg of calcium. But you can get enough calcium without dairy products. While it is not expected that you would eat as much grass and grains as a cow, remember the cow itself does not drink milk yet it gets plenty of calcium in its diet. With so many choices of the following foods, a diet rich in a variety of foods will be able to meet the requirements. Supplements are also an additional option for insurance purposes.

Approximate calcium content (mg)
per 1 cup serving

Dark green leafy vegetables

cooked spinach	250
cooked collards	300
cooked bok choy	330
cooked turnip greens	450
cooked kale	200
parsley	200
cooked mustard greens	180
dandelion greens	150
romaine lettuce	40

Beans and Peas

tofu	150
navy beans	140
soybeans	130
pinto beans	100
garbanzo beans	95
lima, black beans	60
lentils	50
split peas	20

Seafood

raw oysters	240
shrimp	300
salmon with bones	490
mackerel with bones	600
sardines with bones	1,000

Sea vegetables
(seaweed)

nori	1,200
kombu	2,100
wakame	3,500
agar-agar	1,000

Sprouts

soy	50
mung	35
alfalfa	25

Grains

tapioca (dried)	300
brown rice, cooked	20
quinoa, cooked	80
corn meal, whole gr.	50
rye flour, dark	40
oats	40
tortillas (2)	120
whole wheat flour	50

Nuts and Seeds

almonds	750
hazelnuts (filbert)	450
walnuts	280
sesame seeds	2,100
sunflower seeds	260

The following herbs contain variable amounts of calcium:

borage	lamb's quarter
wild lettuce	nettles
burdock	yellow dock

To further support the idea that milk may not be the best source of calcium, a study in 1990 compared the absorption of calcium from kale with the absorption from milk (Heaney and Weaver). The study revealed absorption of calcium from kale was 40.9%, compared with 32.1% from milk.

Choose those green leafy vegetables

As the table above suggests, many dark green leafy vegetables have relatively high calcium concentrations. The calcium in spinach is, however, somewhat poorly absorbed, presumably because of the high concentration of oxalate. The study revealed that kale, a low-oxalate vegetable, is a good source of bioavailable calcium. Kale is a member of the same family that includes broccoli, turnip greens, collard greens and mustard greens. These low-oxalate, calcium-rich vegetables are therefore also likely to be good sources of available calcium. These safer sources of calcium are desirable because milk is a contributing factor in the development of many allergic and autoimmune disorders.

Calcium supplementation:

If you feel you are unable to obtain enough calcium from your diet alone, then you should consider the use a calcium supplement. There are many types of calcium available and many patients have been told by their physician to use an antacid (calcium carbonate) as a calcium source.

I discourage the use of antacids as a source of calcium because they act to reduce the amount of stomach acid. This may eventually reduce the absorption of other minerals and proteins. With so many better products available, the use of a medication for a calcium source seems very unwise.

Calcium carbonate vs. calcium citrate or calcium citrate-malate

While calcium carbonate may be inexpensive, research indicates it may also not be the most effective form of calcium supplementation. There have been numerous studies comparing the absorption of calcium carbonate versus other forms of calcium. Several studies have suggested that in the presence of adequate stomach acid, calcium from the carbonate is absorbed. However, in patients who have reduced stomach acid (those using antacids?), calcium absorption from citrate was superior.

In one study using an oral load technique (Harvey et al.), it was demonstrated that calcium absorption following a 500 mg load of calcium as calcium citrate was higher than after a 2000 mg load of calcium from calcium carbonate. It also suggested that simply using higher doses will not compensate for deficient calcium absorption.

In a group of women who had experienced menopause six or more years earlier and who had low dietary calcium intake, calcium citrate-malate prevented bone loss from the spine, while calcium carbonate did not when compared with use of placebo (Dawson-Hughes et al.). In the same study, use of calcium citrate-malate showed not only significantly less bone loss, but also showed increases in mineralization of bone versus calcium carbonate which did not did not show an increase in bone mineralization.

Calcium hydroxyapatite

Another form of calcium, microcrystalline calcium hydroxyapatite concentrate (MCHC) has been shown effective in the management of osteoporosis. This product is whole bone extract complete with the organic matrix found in raw, young bone. In addition to calcium and protein, it also contains many other trace minerals in the same physiological proportions found in bone. The effectiveness of MCHC in the treatment of osteoporotic postmenopausal women with primary biliary cirrhosis was studied (Epstein et al.) and showed there was an increased bone thickness when supplemented vs the expected typical bone loss in the control group.

From the above studies it is evident that all calciums are not created equal.

Take enough calcium to make up the difference you are receiving from your diet and the following table, depending on your age group.

Group	Milligrams/day
infants, birth to 6 months	400
infants, 6-12 months	600
children (up to 10 years)	800
teens	1200-1500
adults (to age 35)	1200
adults (35-50)	1000
post-menopausal women	1500
men, 51-65	1000
men over 65	1500

The different types of supplements include:

calcium carbonate	highest amount of calcium per pill but may cause intestinal gas and/or constipation, has an antacid effect and interferes with digestion
calcium citrate	less calcium per pill but better absorbed than carbonate; no known side effects
calcium citrate-malate	research suggests this is the best-absorbed form of calcium, can reduce bone loss; with enhanced absorption smaller doses of calcium are needed (Smith et al.)

microcrystalline hydroxyapatite concentrate	well-absorbed calcium source, a complete bone food, can reduce bone loss
calcium phosphate	already too much phosphorus in an average diet so avoid this form
calcium lactate	made from fermentation of molasses, whey, starch or sugar with calcium carbonate
calcium gluconate	requires many pills to get any amount of calcium
dolomite, bone meal	may be contaminated with lead, so know your supplier; not a recommended source

Calcium in the diet and different types of supplements will remain a hot topic. At the present time I suggest you use calcium citrate-malate and calcium hydroxyapatite as supplemental forms of calcium.

References

Dawson-Hughes B, Dallal GE, Krall EA, et al. "A controlled trial of the effect of calcium supplementation on bone density in postmenopausal women." *N Engl J Med* 1990;323:878-883.

Epstein O, et al. "Vitamin D, hydroxyapatite, and calcium gluconate in treatment of cortical bone thinning in postmenopausal women with primary biliary cirrhosis" *Am J Clin Nut* (1982) 36:426-430.

Harvey JA, et al. "Dose dependency of calcium absorption: a comparison of calcium carbonate and calcium citrate." *J Bone Min Res* 3(3):253-258; 1988.

Heaney RP, Weaver CM "Calcium absorption from kale." *Am J Clin Nutr* 1990;51:656-657.

Smith KT et al. "Calcium absorption from a new calcium delivery system(CCM)." *Calcific Tissue Int* 1987;41:351-352.

Appendix Three

Directions For Steaming Vegetables

vegetable	minutes	vegetable	minutes
asparagus	5	mint	1-2
green, lima, stringbeans	5	mushrooms	2
bean sprouts	1-2	mustard, fresh	1-2
beet greens	3-5	okra	5
beets, quartered	15	onions, whole	5
broccoli	5	pea pods	3
brussel sprouts	5	peas	3-5
cabbage, quartered	5	peppers (chili, green,)	2-3
carrots, ½" slices	5	potatoes, sweet, ½"	15
cauliflower, whole	5	potatoes, white, ½"	10
celery	3-5	pumpkin	5
chard	1-2	radishes	5
chicory	1-2	rhubarb	5
chives	2-3	romaine lettuce	1-2
collards	1-2	rutabagas	8
corn, kernels	3	spinach	1-2
dandelion greens	1-2	squash (acorn, spaghetti)	5
eggplant	5	squash (summer, zucchini)	3
garlic	5	tomatoes	3
Jerusalem artichokes	8	turnips, quartered	8
kale	1-2	water chestnuts	8
leeks	5	watercress	1-2

When steaming vegetables, make certain the steamer basket is above the level of the water and the water is boiling rapidly before the vegetables are covered and the timing begins. Once the vegetables are steamed, place them under cold running water. This stops the cooking and preserves the texture and color. The times given above will result in crisp, tender vegetables which have retained much of their nutritional value.

Appendix Four

Corn

Corn is a very widely used ingredient in many processed foods. It is one of the more common food irritants that affect people. Most people think only of corn on the cob, but as the following list suggests, it is widely distributed in many different food products. I have seen it result in a very wide range of symptoms from fatigue to hyperactivity, skin rashes to heart palpitations, headaches to foot cramps. Be very diligent reading for labels which contain any of the following.

There are four basic parts to a corn kernel; starch, germ, gluten and hull. They are all processed into different products.

Starch may become:

basic cornstarch	modified food starch
dextrin	corn syrup (liquid and solid)
maltodextrin	high fructose corn syrup
dextrose	

dextrose may be further processed to produce:

lactic acid	inositol
sorbitol	mannitol
gluconic acid	hydrol (corn-sugar molasses)
caramel color	alcohol

Germ is used for:
corn oil

Gluten is used for:
zein and other protein products

Hull is used for:
bran

Foods Which May Contain Corn

ale
bacon
batters for frying
beers
beverages, carbonated
bourbon/whiskey
burritos
candy
cereals
Cheerios
chow mein
colas
corn flakes
corn toasties
Crackels
cream pies
custards
deep fat frying mixtures
egg nog
fish, prepared/processed
foods, fried
Fritos
fruits — canned, frozen
fruit pies
frying fats
glucose products
grape juice
grits
gin
hominy
ice cream
jellies
Ketchup
Kremel
lemonade
Lifesavers
margarine
Metrecal cookies/wafers
MSG

aspirin and other tablets
baking mixes
bee pollen
beets, Harvard
bleached white flours
breads and pastries
cakes
catsup
cheeses
chop suey
coffee, instant
confectioners' sugar
corn soya
cough syrups
Cream O Soy
cream puffs
dates
dextrose
enchiladas
flour, bleached
french dressing
frostings
fruit juices
fructose
gelatin desserts
graham crackers
gravies
gums, chewing
hams— cured, tenderized
honey
jams
Jell-O
Kix
leavening agents — baking
  powder, yeasts
liquors — ale, beer, gin, whiskey
meats — bacon, bologna, ham,
  luncheon meats, sausages,
  wieners

mull soy
Nescafe
Pablum
peanut butters (some)
pickles
pork and beans
powdered sugar
puddings—custards, Royal
ravioli
salt seasoning, (A & P 4 Seasons)
sandwich spreads
sausages
Similac
soft drinks
soybean milks
string beans—canned, frozen
syrups, commercial—Karo, Cartose, glucose, Puretose, Sweetose
tamales
vegetables—canned, frozen, creamed
vinegar, distilled

Nabisco products
noodles
pastries—cakes, cupcakes
peas, canned
pies, creamed
Post Toasties
preserves
rice, coated
root beer
salad dressing
sauces—meats, fish, sundaes
sherbets
Sobee
soups—creamed, vegetable
spaghetti
sugar, powdered
tortillas

tea, instant
vinegar, distilled

Corn-Free Diet

Food Category	Foods You Can Eat, Unless Sensitive	Foods to Avoid
meat, poultry, fish, vegetable protein	veal, lamb, chicken, fish, turkey, shellfish, dried beans and peas, nuts, nut butters	cold cuts, hams, bacon, sausages, wieners
dairy products	milk in glass containers, cottage cheese	milk in waxed paper cartons, ice cream, sherbet
eggs	any form, yolk or white	eggnog
grain products	corn-free cereals	Cornflakes, Rice Krispies, CornChex, Kix, Cheerios

	whole grain bread spaghetti, noodles, macaroni	graham crackers coated rice
soups	broth	cream soups, vegetable soup
fruit	fresh	canned with "sugar added"
vegetables	fresh or frozen (except corn)	Harvard beets, canned peas, canned vegetables, frozen vegetables in waxed containers, succotash
desserts	all that do not contain corn	cakes, cookies, cream pies
sweets	candy	
beverages	vegetable juice (fresh), herbal teas, mineral water, filtered water, unsweetened fruit juice, chicory and dandelion roots, Roma, Cafix, Inka, Roastaroma, Caffree	beers, whiskies, fruit juice, carbonated drinks, soybean milks
oils	olive, canola, flax, sesame, sunflower	corn oil, salad dressings with corn oil
miscellaneous	sea salt, spices, wheat-free, corn-free baking powder	salt, catsup, peanut butter, chewing gum, popcorn, distilled vinegar

With each of these suggestions please be sure to read labels carefully. As food companies become more aware of the problems people are having with more and more foods, they are making acceptable substitution products.

Appendix Five

Eggs

A common ingredient in many baked products, I have often found eggs a problem in many young children with atopic dermatitis (eczema). Excessive flatulence is another common problem which has responded to removal of eggs from the diet.

The following foods may contain eggs and should be avoided on an egg-free diet.

angel cake
baking powders
batters for french frying
bavarian cream
bouillon
breads
cakes
candies
consommés
cocoa drinks
cookies
creamed pies
croquettes
custards
dessert powders
doughnuts
dumplings
egg in any form—
  creamed, deviled, dried,
  fried, hard boiled, poached
fritters
frostings
french toast
griddle cakes
glazed rolls
hamburger mix

meat loaf
meat jellies
meringues
muffins
noodles
omelets
Ovaltine
Ovomalt
pastes
pancakes
patties
pie fillings
puddings
pretzels
root beer
salad dressings
sauces
sausages
sherbets
soufflés
soups
spaghetti
Spanish creams
sponge cakes
tartar sauce
timbales

hollandaise sauce
ice cream
icings
macaroons
macaroni

waffles
waffle mixes
whips
wines (many)
marshmallows

Egg Substitutes (for cooking)

1 whole egg =	2 Tbsp. liquid + 2 Tbsp. flour + ½ Tbsp. fat + ½ tsp. baking powder
or	1 Tbsp. ground flax or psyllium seeds and 3 Tbsp. of water
or	Ener-G Foods Egg Replacer™ (contains potato flour)

Egg-free Diet

Food Category	Foods You Can Eat, Unless Sensitive	Foods to Avoid
meat, poultry, fish, vegetable protein	veal, lamb, chicken, fish, turkey, shellfish dried beans and peas, nuts, nut butters	any meat mixture with egg (meat balls, hamburger, croquettes, meat loaf
dairy products	milk, cheese	any cheese mixtures containing eggs, ice cream, sherbet
eggs	Ener-G Egg Replacer™ (not Egg Beaters™)	any form, yolk or white, powdered eggs
grain products	all cereals, most bread and rolls, french bread unless glazed with egg white, eggless pasta	any bread with eggs, griddle cakes, pretzels, waffles, pancakes, muffins, noodles, spaghetti, macaroni containing eggs

soups	all soups not including egg as a thickener or cleared with egg	bouillon, consommé, noodle soup, mock turtle soup, egg drop soup
vegetables	fresh or frozen	vegetable soufflés
fruit	fresh	
desserts	all that do not contain eggs	pudding, meringues, cakes, cream pies, cake flour, cookies, icing, doughnuts, custards, macaroons
sweets		candy
beverages	vegetable juice (fresh), herbal teas, mineral water, filtered water, unsweetened fruit juice, chicory and dandelion roots, Roma, Cafix, Inka, Roastaroma, Caffree	malted drinks, Ovaltine, Ovomalt, wine (clarified with eggs), eggnogs, root beer
oils	olive, canola, flax, sesame, sunflower	
miscellaneous	sea salt, spices, wheat-free, corn-free baking powder	mayonnaise, hollandaise sauce, tartar sauce, baking powder

With each of these suggestions please be sure to read labels carefully. As food companies become more aware of the problems people are having with more and more foods, they are making acceptable substitution products.

Appendix Six

Fats and Oils

Much of America is conscious of the discussion about fat in the typical diet. Misinformation about fats and oils dates back to 1960s when the American Heart Association proclaimed that saturated fat and cholesterol lead to hardening of the arteries and heart disease. As a result, many people switched from saturated animal fats like butter and lard to cholesterol-free margarine and greatly increased the use of polyunsaturated vegetable oils. It is highly advertised and recommended that you choose a diet with as little fat as possible. High fat diets are associated with a number of diseases, including heart disease and breast cancer. Most recommendations suggest that total saturated fats be reduced to about 10% of energy intake, but the optimal level may be much lower.

Fatty acids are important

Fats and oils are made of building blocks called fatty acids. There are two essential fatty acids which must be obtained from foods because the body cannot make them. They are known as cis-linoleic acid (LA) and alpha-linolenic acid (LNA). This means that some fat is essential in the diet for optimal health. However, different fatty acids have different effects on human health and many people focus on reducing fat without consideration as to specific types of fat.

The fatty acids are known as saturated fatty acids, mono-unsaturated fatty acids (omega 9), polyunsaturated fatty acids (omega 6), (super)polyunsaturated fatty acids (omega 3). The omega 3 fatty acids promote health and help prevent degenerative diseases. However, even though the average American diet gets 37% of calories from fats, it usually contains insufficient amounts of omega 3 oils and excessive amounts of saturated fats from animal (non-fish) sources.

The following chart shows the breakdown of fats in several different vegetable oils. (Information obtained from Omega Nutrition.)

Oil	Saturated	Omega 9	Omega 6	Omega 3
Almond	9%	65%	26%	
Brazil nuts	23%	29%	45%	
Coconut	89%	9%		
Canola	6%	60%	24%	10%
Flax	9%	18%	16%	57%
Hazelnut	7%	76%	15%	
Olive	10%	82%	8%	
Pistachio	12%	54%	31%	
Pumpkin	20%	20%	60%	
Safflower	8%	13%	79%	
Sunflower	8%	19%	69%	
Sesame	13%	46%	41%	
Walnut	16%	28%	51%	5%

Unfortunately, many people are deceived by all the advertising they are constantly exposed to. They are led to believe that if they choose no-fat or low-fat foods, they will be reducing fats to healthy levels. Foods high in omega 3 fatty acids need to be increased or added to the average diet while saturated fats need to be avoided or decreased. Total fat intake needs to be decreased but not at the expense of the healthy type of fats.

Many children with eczema, allergies and asthma have responded to the addition of essential fatty acids to their diet. Adults with dry skin, rheumatoid arthritis, hypertension, or diabetes, women with premenstrual tension and men with benign prostatic hypertrophy do well when healthy fats become an essential part of their diet.

Saturated fats

Saturated fats worsen diabetes, bursitis, arthritis, tendinitis, allergies, asthma and blood pressure. The main sources are dairy products, red meat and lard. Saturated fats are typically considered to be "bad" fat, but a more appropriate word may be "land-mammal fat." If your diet includes such foods as beef, lamb, pork, butter, lard, eggs, cheese, milk, poultry, ice cream, and processed foods you are likely consuming excessive quantities of saturated fat.

Coconut oil

Oils from tropical plants, such as coconut oil and palm-kernel oil are also saturated fats but are minor components of the present U.S. food supply. Many years ago coconut oil was implicated in raising cholesterol levels when ingested. It is now known that the reason for this was because of the presence of trans-fatty acids and a lack of essential fatty acids in the coconut oil that was used. Any diet which includes hydrogenated products always results in high serum cholesterol levels because these products contain harmful trans-fatty acids and lack healthy essential fatty acids.

Unrefined coconut oil is non-hydrogenated, naturally saturated, contains no trans-fatty acids and is solid at room temperature. This may make it an acceptable alternative to butter or margarine. In addition it contains medium chain saturates (distinct from long chain saturates in animal products which are associated with "bad" cholesterol), which research shows do not clog arteries. In fact, these medium chain fatty acids are easier to digest for people who have problems digesting fats, and can be converted to energy rather than stored as fat. Coconut oil also contains lauric acid, a disease-fighting fatty acid. Found naturally in breast milk, lauric acid helps infants from being infected by many viruses and a few bacteria.

Unsaturated fats

Unsaturated fats contain essential fatty acids which are necessary in the diet. They help regulate the immune system, reduce inflammation, minimize allergies, help control blood pressure and reduce triglyceride levels. They are found in such foods as whole grains, nuts, seeds, oils, and cold water fish.

Omega 3 fatty acids

Salmon, trout, mackerel, sardines, oils of cold water fish, and flax seed oil contain high amounts of omega 3 fatty acids. They should be included in your diet. There are a number of different ways to incorporate flax seed oil into your diet. Try several of the following ideas.

Flax seed oil recipes

Fresh flax seed oil, besides its nutritionally unique composition of essential fatty acids, has a pleasing (for some), light, nutty flavor.

It can replace less nutritious oils in all ways that oil is used, except for frying. Frying destroys the healthful properties of this oil. When using flax seed oil in hot foods (soups, cooked or steamed vegetables, etc.), add the oil last, just before or after serving.

Probably the best way to use flax seed oil is in cold dishes, the most nutritionally balanced and versatile of which is the following oil-protein mixture.

Basic Flax Oil-Protein Mixture

40 grams (3 Tbsp.) fresh flax seed oil
100 grams (7 Tbsp.) soy yogurt or soft tofu

Mix thoroughly. This oil-protein mixture can be eaten as is, or converted into any number of nutritious and tasty dishes. Here are some suggestions:

Breakfast

For a delicious and strength-giving breakfast, add to the basic mixture:

— a touch of maple syrup or honey

— freshly ground nuts or seeds (almonds, filberts, flax, walnuts, sunflower seeds and sesame seeds) or even granola

— fruit juice or cut fresh fruit in season (strawberry, raspberry, apple, pear, peach, apricot, plum, blueberry, huckleberry, etc.)

Main Meal

For a nourishing and health-building main dish for lunch or supper, add to the basic mixture:

— finely shredded green onions and parsley

— grated carrots, green and red peppers, cut tomatoes, and/or any other fresh vegetables

—herbs and seasonings of your choice: basil, tarragon, thyme, oregano, cumin, coriander, marjoram, curry, dill, etc. There are many possible combinations.

Salad Dressing

Add to the basic mixture: vinegar, soy sauce or tamari, your choice of spices and herbs (garlic, mustard, hot spices, basic, cumin, dill, thyme, coriander, oregano, parsley, onion, green onion, etc.) and blend. Makes a creamy, flavorful, and very nutritious dressing.

Mayonnaise

This recipe is foolproof if followed exactly (don't try to double it!) Set aside ½ cup flax seed oil and ½ cup oil of your choice (safflower, sunflower, or olive). Break an egg into the blender, add 2 tablespoons lemon juice or vinegar, a dash of mustard (dry or prepared), a dash of cayenne or ground white pepper, and ¼ cup of oil. Cover blender and begin to blend at low speed until it begins to thicken. Immediately add the remaining ¾ cup oil in a heavy stream while continuing to blend at low speed. This makes 1½ cups.

Dessert

Simply add fruits, nuts, and/or sweeteners in varying proportions to your taste.

Butter Lovers

You can greatly improve the nutritional value of butter — which is very low in essential fatty acids and contains cholesterol — by mixing butter and fresh flax seed oil in 1:1 proportions. This softens the butter, adds a delicious flavor, and supplies cholesterol-lowering EFAs to the butter-fat. Remember to refrigerate it. (See also "Better Butter" on page 123.)

Olive Oil Lovers

You can mix olive oil and flax seed oil 1:1. This will retain the olive oil's flavor and greatly enhance its nutritional value.

You can also use it:

— on cooked or steamed vegetables, instead of melted butter, a more healthful choice

— on baked potatoes instead of sour cream

— in protein shakes and smoothies

— as the best massage and tanning oil available
(Be sure to take appropriate care with fabrics.)

Because essential fatty acids (EFAs) increase the metabolic rate, EFA-rich flax oil is less likely than any other oil to result in weight gain. In fact, studies have shown that many overweight people actually lose weight by adding this fresh essential fatty acid-rich oil to their diet.

Omega 6 fatty acids

Safflower and sunflower oils contain the highest amounts of omega 6 fatty acids while soybean oil, wheat germ oil and sesame seed oil contain lesser amounts. Some people will be familiar with encapsulated omega 6 oils as evening primrose oil, borage oil and black currant seed oil.

You are more likely to be deficient in omega 3 fatty acids than omega 6 fatty acids because of the heavy use of vegetable oils, and the only concentrated sources of omega 3 fatty acids are flaxseed and oily fish which are not eaten nearly as frequently.

Quality of the oil is key

Be careful of poor-quality polyunsaturated oils which food manufacturers advertise widely. Corn, safflower, sunflower and other vegetable oils known as polyunsaturates and sold in clear glass containers are usually ruined by processing. The seeds are crushed under enormous pressure and cooked at high temperatures, the oil is then processed with chemical solvents and caustic substances, bleached and deodorized. The result is a bland, colorless oil stripped of all its nutrients. These oils may be rapidly degraded or oxidized by exposure to light, heat and air. They are usually sold in clear bottles which allows light through and oxidation to occur. Eating these damaged oils can harm your circulatory system.

Trans fatty acids: problems

It is now evident that we should avoid products like margarine and other processed foods such as chips, crackers and cookies because of the presence of trans fatty acids. These unhealthy fatty acids are created when the liquid polyunsaturated oils are hydrogenated by bubbling hydrogen through the oils to make them solid and increase their shelf life. These synthetic fatty acids make up as much as 35% of the fats in some stick margarine and can compete with natural fatty acids. Hydrogenating a "good" vegetable oil chemically alters its naturally occurring fatty acids to form unnatural fat molecules that affects the way in which the body burns these fats.

Some research now indicates that trans fatty acids may double the risk of a heart attack. Researcher Mary Enig reports that trans fatty acids contribute to cancer, diabetes, obesity, and may adversely affect reproduction and lactation.

They should be considered suspect until proved innocent. As a result, switching to margarine is not recommended as a means to try to reduce your risk of heart disease.

Use "Better Butter"

In place of margarine or shortening, use olive oil or small amounts of "better butter." You can make your own "better butter" according to the following recipe.

Blend ¼ cup of softened or warmed butter with ⅛ to ½ cup of oil such as olive, sunflower or safflower. The best oils are organic, unrefined, unhydrogenated, cold, expeller (mechanically) pressed without solvents and stored in opaque containers protected from light, oxygen and heat. They should be refrigerated and consumed fresh before going rancid or spoiling.

You may add 1-2 tablespoons of flax seed oil to "better butter," or capsules of vitamin E, evening primrose oil, borage oil, or black currant seed oil. You may also choose to spice up your own "better butter" recipe with garlic, chili pepper, tarragon, sage, rosemary, thyme, lemon, honey, vanilla, or any spice of your choice. Be creative and try a different recipe each time you make up a new batch. It is important to remember though that there is saturated fat in "better butter" so use it sparingly. (See also "Butter Lovers" on page 121.)

Olive oil is still the number one choice

The best oil to consistently use is olive oil which contains oleic acid, a mono-unsaturated fatty acid, which is more stable at high temperatures and less prone to oxidation than other vegetables oils. It has not been implicated in heart disease or cancer, which are two of the main health problems associated with fats and oils. Buy "extra virgin" which is top quality or "virgin" but not "pure" olive oil which is a blend of oils. To test whether you have true olive oil or a blend, refrigerate the container, if the oil solidifies, it's the real thing.

Canola oil

Canola oil is high in mono-unsaturated fatty acids, is light, and doesn't have a heavy taste; but it's usually refined like other vegetable oils — a poor second choice to extra virgin olive oil.

Sources of superior oils

Some of the best oils to buy are produced by Omega Nutrition, Bellingham, WA and by Flora Inc., Lynden, WA. Their unrefined oils are made from certified organic seeds, pressed in small batches, protected from light and heat and processed without chemicals or preservatives. The extra cost is well worth it for your health.

The optimal diet has about 10% fat obtained from foods which contain the essential fatty acids mentioned above. If you choose mostly low fat items from the list below, you can be confident that your diet will fall within the ideal guidelines.

Low fat (less than 10%)

beans: lentils, pinto, black
whole wheat bread
barley, buckwheat, spelt, teff
most vegetables
potatoes
tuna packed in water

puffed cereals
white turkey meat
most fruits
flake cereals
rice
pretzels

10% — 30% fat

bluefish
scallops
low-fat yogurt
buttermilk
beef liver
onion soup
pea soup
oysters
lobster
low-fat cottage cheese

King crab
pancakes
low-fat milk
mussels
plain bran cereals
plain popcorn
chicken breast
oatmeal
collard greens
saltines

30% — 40% fat

tuna packed in oil
cheese crackers
beef gravy
flank steak
trout
cheese pizza
sirloin steak
pink salmon, canned

rump roast
bran muffins
waffles
french fries
chicken wings
white perch
loin lamb chops

40% — 50% fat

porterhouse steak
sardines
lean ground beef
ice cream

ham
part-skim ricotta cheese
whole milk

More than 50% fat

avocados	margarine
butter	spareribs
nuts	sour cream
cream cheese	peanut butter
sausage	heavy cream
most hard cheeses	chocolate
blue cheese dressing	potato chips
eggs	brie cheese
bacon	oil-based dressings
mayonnaise	hot dogs

How to reduce saturated fats in your diet

Some of the best ways to reduce saturated fat intake include:

* Avoid or reduce the consumption of red meats, organ meats, eggs, dairy products and processed foods. If you choose to eat animal meats, use the leanest cuts and trim excess fats, including poultry fat and the skin. Even though you have trimmed away obvious fat, there will be significant amounts of fat present.

* Choose protein sources such as fish and legumes.

* Broil, bake, boil or water-sauté foods instead of frying. To water-sauté food instead of stir-frying in oil, put ½ to 1 cup of water into a wok or skillet and bring to a rapid boil. Quickly add the vegetables and keep stirring over high heat until done.

Omega 3 and Omega 6 fatty acids

To increase omega 3 and omega 6 fatty acids in your diet:

* Use flax seed oil as a healthy dressing for your vegetables, grains, lentils and legumes. You may mix it into your hot foods (oatmeal, pasta, baked potato, etc.), but never cook with it (because the heat destroys the omega 3 fatty acids).

If you do not like the taste on your food, then adults can take 1-2 tablespoons, children 2-4 teaspoons per day and wash it down with water or juice. Divide the doses and take before your meals.

* Grind flax and sesame seeds and sprinkle them on top of your foods. Since they are too small to chew, it is important to grind them to break the husks and thus maximize their breakdown to ensure proper absorption. You should eat 2-4 tablespoons a day.

* Add sunflower, pumpkin seeds and fresh walnuts as snacks.

* Add legumes to your diet, as they provide important B vitamins and essential amino acids.

* Include salmon, mackerel, trout and sardines in your diet. With so much concern about the potential of toxic residues, it is important to not eat the same fish frequently so use variety. It is also a good idea to buy the fish from different stores.

* Have at least one cup of dark leafy green vegetables (spinach, parsley, broccoli, seaweed, etc.) a day. Use a wide variety of vegetables and do not eat the same ones over and over. It is always possible to invent a salad. You may also stir-fry (in water), steam, or bake the vegetables.

* Add home grown sprouts to salads. They provide many valuable nutrients and essential fatty acids. See the section on preparation of sprouts, page 176.

Many people are aware of the connection between high cholesterol levels and the increased risk of cardio-vascular disease. The following table is a list of foods which contain the highest amounts of cholesterol.

Cholesterol Content of Common Foods
(milligrams)

liver, beef	545
McDonald's Scrambled Eggs	399
McDonald's Egg McMuffin	226
shrimp (4 oz)	220
egg (1 large)	213
Burger King Whopper w/cheese	113
beef, pork, lamb, trimmed (4 oz)	104
chicken, turkey, skinned (4 oz)	87-101
flounder, sole, clams (4 oz)	76
ice cream, vanilla (¾ cup)	66
egg noodles (1 cup)	50
cheddar cheese (1½ oz)	45
milk, whole (1 cup)	33
cottage cheese, creamed or 4% (½ cup)	24
yogurt, non-fat or partially skimmed (1 cup)	17
butter, salted (1 pat)	11
mayonnaise (1 Tbsp.)	8
egg white (1 large)	0
beans, fruit, vegetables (except avocado)	0

The optimal intake of cholesterol is probably zero, meaning the avoidance of animal products. In regard to coronary heart disease, obesity, which is primarily an exercise-deficiency syndrome, is likely as important a contributor as the composition of our diets. Other aspects of the diet, such as antioxidants (vitamin A, C and E, selenium) and other micronutrients may also be very important in preventing coronary artery disease. New research indicates that homocysteine levels are another important indicator in heart disease. Adequate amounts of B vitamins — especially folic acid, B12 and B6 — will be protective.

Animal fats

By minimizing (eliminating?) the use of animal foods such as meat, poultry, seafood and dairy products, you can significantly reduce the amount of cholesterol (and fat) you consume. Egg yolks, shrimp and organ meats are especially high in cholesterol. Reducing cholesterol levels can be especially important in patients with a history of cardiovascular problems, high blood pressure, diabetes, gallbladder problems, and degenerative arthritis.

If you are eating many of the above foods and have a high cholesterol level, you should see a dramatic drop of 20-30% within four weeks. If you don't, your dietary changes are probably not radical enough.

I have had many frustrated patients who have tried very hard to change their diet to decrease their fat intake only to find no change in their cholesterol level. If you have a family history of high cholesterol you may have a condition known as familial hyperlipidemia. This can been measured with a special blood test. If this is the problem it needs to be approached differently than by simple reduction of fat in the diet.

Appendix Seven

Fiber

While not considered essential to the body, fiber's presence in our diet may reduce the incidence of obesity, diverticulosis, constipation, hemorrhoids, and varicose veins.

What is fiber?

Dietary fiber is the part of food that is not digested by enzymes in the small intestine, where most food is digested and absorbed. While some types of dietary fiber make it through the body undigested, other types are broken down by bacteria in the large intestine. The products of this breakdown include methane, carbon dioxide, water and volatile fatty acids, all of which may cause gas or bloating in some people.

Different types of fiber

Dietary fiber can be divided into insoluble and soluble fiber.

The *insoluble fibers,* including cellulose, hemicellulose, and lignin, come from the walls of plant cells, and are found in whole grains, beans and other plant products. Wheat bran is far and away the richest source of insoluble fiber. Those intolerant to wheat should use oat bran and rice bran. Insoluble fiber speeds the movement of food through the digestive tract, and because this fiber absorbs water, it increases fecal bulk and contributes to regularity. It's primarily these properties that make insoluble fiber in the diet a useful hedge against constipation and diverticulosis. Diets rich in insoluble fiber can prevent or control other digestive disorders, such as colon cancer, irritable bowel syndrome, Crohn's disease, and ulcerative colitis.

In contrast to insoluble fibers, *soluble* fibers hold water, but do not increase fecal bulk. That's because they are completely digested and absorbed in the large intestine. They do not prevent constipation or other digestive disorders, but they do have a vital role to play.

Soluble fibers help control diabetes and hypoglycemia by preventing dramatic swings in blood sugar levels. These fibers tend to form gels which delay the absorption of nutrients from the intestine. While nutrients in foods low in soluble fibers pass quickly from the beginning of the small intestine into the blood, nutrients in high fiber foods are absorbed slowly over the entire length of the small intestine. This slowed absorption makes it easier for diabetics to keep pace with the influx of carbohydrates into the body.

Soluble fibers also lower blood cholesterol levels, causing a decrease in "bad" low-density lipoprotein (LDL) cholesterol and an increase in "good" high-density lipoprotein (HDL) cholesterol. Researchers are unsure how this happens.

Soluble fibers include gums, mucilages, pectins, and storage polysaccharides. Beans, fruits, and oat bran are good sources of soluble fibers, although most plant foods contain both types of fiber.

The average Western diet contains about 20 grams of dietary fiber per day. It is recommended that people eat 30-40 grams per day.

Meats, milk products, eggs, and fats and oils are not listed in the following food fiber chart because they are virtually devoid of fiber content.

Making sure your diet contains adequate amounts of the "right" kind of fiber is an important part of your overall dietary plan.

Fiber Content of Selected Foods

	serving size	total fiber (grams)	soluble fiber (grams)	insoluble fiber (grams)
Vegetables				
peas	½ cup	5.2	2.0	3.2
parsnips	½ cup	4.4	0.4	4.0
potatoes	1 small	3.8	2.2	1.6
broccoli	½ cup	2.6	1.6	1.0
zucchini	½ cup	2.5	1.1	1.4
squash, summer	½ cup	2.3	1.1	1.2
carrots	½ cup	2.2	1.5	0.7
tomatoes	½ cup	2.0	0.6	1.4
brussel sprouts	½ cup	1.8	0.7	1.1
beans, string	½ cup	1.7	0.6	1.1
onions	½ cup	1.6	0.8	0.8
rutabagas	½ cup	1.6	0.7	0.9
beets	½ cup	1.5	0.6	0.9
kale greens	½ cup	1.4	0.6	0.8
turnips	½ cup	1.3	0.6	0.7
asparagus	½ cup	1.2	0.3	0.9
eggplant	½ cup	1.2	0.7	0.5
radishes	½ cup raw	1.2	0.3	0.9
cauliflower	½ cup	0.9	0.3	0.6
beans, sprouted	½ cup	0.9	0.3	0.6
cucumber	½ cup raw	0.8	0.5	0.3
lettuce	½ cup raw	0.5	0.2	0.3
Fruits				
apple	1 small	3.9	2.3	1.6
blackberries	½ cup	3.7	0.7	3.0
pear	1 small	2.5	0.6	1.9
strawberries	¾ cup	2.4	0.9	1.5
plums	2 med.	2.3	1.3	1.0
tangerine	1 med.	1.8	1.4	0.4
apricots	2 med.	1.3	0.9	0.4
banana	1 small	1.3	0.6	0.7
grapefruit	½	1.3	0.9	0.4
peaches	1 medium	1.0	0.5	0.5

cherries	10	0.9	0.3	0.6
pineapple	½ cup	0.8	0.2	0.6
grapes	10	0.4	0.1	0.3

Breads, Cereals

bran (100%)	½ cup*	10.0	0.3	9.7
popcorn	3 cups	2.8	0.8	2.0
rye bread	1 slice	2.7	0.8	1.9
whole grain bread	1 slice	2.7	0.08	2.6
rye wafers	3	2.3	0.06	2.2
corn grits	½ cup*	1.9	0.6	1.3
oats, whole	½ cup*	1.6	0.5	1.1
graham crackers	2	1.4	0.04	1.4
brown rice	½ cup	1.3	0	1.3
french bread	1 slice	1.0	0.4	0.6
dinner roll	1	0.8	0.03	0.8
egg noodles	½ cup*	0.8	0.03	0.8
spaghetti	½ cup	0.8	0.02	0.8
white bread	1 slice	0.8	0.03	0.8
white rice	½ cup*	0.5	0	0.5

Legumes

kidney beans	½ cup*	4.5	0.5	4.0
white beans	½ cup*	4.2	0.4	3.8
pinto beans	½ cup*	3.0	0.3	2.7
lima beans	½ cup*	1.4	0.2	1.2

Nuts

almonds	10	1.0	
peanuts	10	1.0	
walnuts, black	1 tsp.	0.6	
pecans	2	0.5	

* indicates cooked

Constipation is a very common presenting complaint. If we study diet and bowel habits in native Africa we find that they have a large bulky stool after every main meal. This is far from what I find in practice. Some patients have fewer than three bowels movements a month!

These patients will tell you they have tried everything. The most commonly tried suggestions are more water and the addition of Metamucil™. Because of the high sugar content in this product, I do not recommend its use. There are many other ideas which must be followed to correct this problem, including a complete overview of the diet.

You should see a Naturopathic physician to help deal with this persistent problem if your own home remedies have not helped the problem.

Appendix Eight

Food Additives

A food additive is a substance that is added to food in connection with its processing, packaging, transportation or preparation for some purpose other than nutrition. In general, substances are added to food to perform the following functions:

1. to add or enhance flavor

2. to add or enhance color

3. to modify or maintain texture or consistency

4. to modify its maturation rate

5. to act as a preservative in preventing spoilage

6. to aid in the manufacturing process

They provide no nutritional value to the food and generally should be avoided or at least minimized, whether you are sensitive or not. The more whole foods you choose to eat, the better will be your nutritional status.

There are more than 3500 substances being added to foods. Of these, only about 10% need to be listed on the label. Below are listed just a few of the thousands of products available for use in the food supply.

Sodium nitrate, sodium nitrite

This is used as a preservative and color stabilizer, maintaining the red color of meats.

processed meats	bacon
wieners	sausages
sandwich meats	processed poultry

Benzoic Acid

This retards & controls the growth of yeast, molds, and some bacteria.

carbonated drinks	fruit juices
cider	margarine
pie fillings	prepared salads

Parabens, PHB ester

These are chemically related to benzoic acid, and are active against yeast and molds.

beer	soft drinks
pastries	cakes
pie crusts	icing
salad dressings	jams
jellies	preserves

Sorbic acid

This is used for molds, yeast, and many bacteria.

cheese	cheese products
fruit drinks	beverage syrups
unsalted margarine	dried fruits
cakes	icing
dips	

Tartrazine (yellow dye #5)

This is a dye (FD & C Yellow # 5), commonly added to "improve" the appearance of a food. It is very important to read labels carefully.

The following is a short list which is suggestive of the thousands of products containing this food dye.

sweet breads	butter
colored cereals	cheeses
some frozen fish	some canned fruits
ice creams	Jell-O (gelatin)

margarine	prepared meats
mustard	pudding
toothpaste	yogurt
baked goods	candies
lozenges	mouthwash
chips (potato, corn, taco)	prepared sauces

Food coloring (in general)

beverages:	most fruit type drinks
	cherries in fruit cocktail
bakery products:	dough products
	cookies
	icings
	coatings
	ice cream cones
candy:	wide variety, most
dairy products:	most ice creams and sherbets
	cheese
	margarine and butter
dry mix products:	gelatin desserts
	puddings
	cakes mixes
	doughnut mixes
	pancake mixes
pet food:	some
meats:	sausage

Sulfites

Sulfites are used as food preservatives to prevent microbial spoilage. They also act as antioxidants to prevent lettuces and other fruits and vegetables from going brown. After a sulfite treatment, vegetables maintain their fresh appearance even though they may be quite old and stale. They are also used to sanitize containers in the fermentation industry. Restaurant meals may contain up to 25-100 mg of metabisulfite in one meal.

There are actually six sulfating agents. These are:

sulphur dioxide
sodium sulfite
sodium bisulfite
potassium bisulfite
sodium metabisulfite
potassium metabisulfite

Some of the most common foods containing sulfites include:

Drinks
commercial bottled drinks containing soft drinks or fruit juice
cordials   beer
champagne   wines
cider with preservatives

Fruit:
dried fruits such as apples, apricots, pears, fruit bars

Vegetables
dried vegetables, including commercially prepared potatoes
pickles, pickled onions   sauerkraut

Meat/Fish/Poultry
sausages, frankfurters   chicken loaf
uncooked fresh prawns (shrimp) shellfish

Dairy products
cheese mixtures and pastes   fruit yogurt

Other
dessert toppings, flavorings relish
jams   some breads
olives   frozen pizzas
tomato puree   tomato paste
some crackers and cookies   sweet pastries

Migraine headaches, flushed skin, upset stomach and diarrhea have all commonly been reported by patients with this intolerance.

I had one patient who experienced a seizure. After an extensive neurological workup, the neurologist determined the only likely cause was the ingestion of sulfite in some shrimp the patient had eaten.

Because of the extreme nature of the reaction, he wrote the Food and Drug administration voicing his grave concern about this product being added to so many foods. The response from the FDA was not very reassuring. Because fewer than fifty deaths had been reported from this product, it was not felt necessary to warn the general population about the potential danger of this product being widely used in so many foods.

This is just another lesson that you need to look out for yourself and can not expect any government agency to make the best decisions for your health.

Monosodium glutamate (MSG)

Monosodium glutamate is added to thousands of products, primarily as a flavor enhancer. Originally obtained from seaweed or soybean, it may now be manufactured by a chemical process from wheat, corn or sugarbeet by-products. Because of this, manufacturers advertise it as a natural substance.

Although glutamate is an amino acid (substances found in all proteins), when MSG is removed from its natural food, it has no nutritional value. Glutamic acid is one of the amino acids which make up proteins. In nature, the glutamic acid is linked to other amino acids. When a person eats a protein substance, the amino acids are slowly broken apart during digestion. When pure MSG is ingested, a rapid effect occurs from the glutamate. The glutamate is not attached to other amino acids and is rapidly absorbed producing blood levels eight to ten times normal. Once ingested, the effects of MSG are widespread throughout the body. Some people are highly sensitive and it may be related to a dose tolerance. It seems the body may attempt to handle the MSG as if it were a foreign substance. MSG has been known to cause "Chinese Restaurant Syndrome," which may result in flushing, headache, a burning sensation in the neck and tightness of the chest.

I have seen many other reactions from MSG, some of which include: asthma, runny nose, rapid heartbeat, chest pain, joint pain, muscle weakness, dizziness, anxiety, hyperactivity, depression, migraine headaches, anger, diarrhea, irritable bowel, hives, and blurred vision.

A *Sixty Minutes* television report cited several studies which showed the adverse effects of this chemical. Despite the studies, the Food and Drug Administration believes that MSG poses no health problems and prefers to ignore the complaints of millions of Americans.

Sure to contain MSG

When used in its pure form it must be labeled as "monosodium glutamate." However, it can be a component of other substances and then on labels, MSG may be hidden under different names.

glutamate (e.g. monopotassium glutamate)

hydrolyzed protein contains 8-40% free glutamate

sodium caseinate or calcium caseinate

autolyzed yeast or yeast extract

Likely to contain MSG

texturized protein	carrageenan
seasonings	natural flavorings
bouillon	broth or stock

| chicken, beef or | malt flavor |
| pork flavor | |

I have had the pleasure of meeting Mr. J. Wayne Erickson of Anchorage, Alaska, and his daughter, who are on a personal crusade to have MSG removed from all food products. Because of a near life-threatening reaction from this compound, he is devoting his retired life to find out everything he can about this unhealthy product. Along with his daughter, a journalism major, they are completing a documentary outlining the dangers of this substance.

Mr. Erickson has extensive knowledge of this subject and I am hopeful that his tireless efforts will soon be recognized, which will then benefit our entire population.

This is definitely a product you should do everything you can to avoid. Read all labels carefully.

Appendix Nine

Legumes

Many people ignore this incredibly nutritious food family because of their reputation for producing gas when eaten. Prepared correctly and seasoned tastefully, they will provide a wonderful nutritional boost to any diet. There is a wide variety available to choose from.

Preparation and cooking suggestions

After you have purchased the beans, sort and rinse them to remove any tiny stones or discolored beans. You have two methods of preparation to choose from. The slow method which will increase the digestibility of the beans and the Quick method for those on the run.

Slow method

Soak one cup of dried legumes in pure, non-chlorinated water overnight (or longer — up to 48 hours is good) in the refrigerator. Cover the legumes with enough water to cover them by at least 2-3 inches. Add more water as the beans expand. Soaking the beans allows enzymes found in them time to break down the gas-producing starches, simplifying digestion. Dried legumes will double or triple in volume by the time they are cooked. One cup of dried beans can provide a meal for 2-4 people.

After soaking the legumes, pour the soaking water on your plants. Place the beans in a cooking pot, add as much fresh cold water as is called for in the cooking directions. Bring to a boil slowly.

Turn down the heat and simmer, partially covered, until soft, according to the table page 144. They should be tender, not mushy. A two-inch piece of kombu (seaweed) added to the beans while cooking will speed up the cooking time and add minerals to the beans as well as lightly salting them. When ready to eat, they should be crushable when placed between your tongue and the roof of your mouth.

Serve them with brown rice, quinoa, millet or other cooked grain, bread or tortillas to make a complete protein meal.

Quick method

No soaking time is required (but you will increase the likelihood of gas). This is especially useful for black-eyed peas and lentils.

After rinsing, place the legumes in a cooking pot. Add enough water to cover the legumes with several inches of water and bring to a boil.

Boil for several moments, then turn off the heat and let sit for at least 2 hours.

After soaking, drain the water, add new water and simmer for 30-45 minutes or until tender.

Cooking Times For Beans

Legume (1 cup dry)	Water	Cooking time	Yield
Azuki beans	2 cups	50 min	2 cups
Black beans	4 cups	1½ hrs	2 cups
Black-eyed peas	2 cups	1 hr	2 cups
Garbanzo (chickpeas)	4 cups	3 hrs	2 cups
Kidney beans	3 cups	1½ hrs	2 cups
Lentils and split peas	3 cups	40-60 min	2¼ cups
Lima beans	2 cups	2½ hrs	1¼ cups
Mung beans	3 cups	2½ hrs	2 cups
Navy beans	2 cups	1½- 2 hrs	2 cups
Pinto beans	3 cups	2½ hrs	2 cups
Red beans	3 cups	3 hrs	2 cups
Small white beans	3 cups	1½ hrs	2 cups
Soybeans	4 cups	3-4 hrs	2 cups

Appendix Ten

Menu Ideas, Meal Planning

Making changes in your diet can seem overwhelming at first. We are very fortunate to have many substitute foods to choose from as we minimize the foods to which we may be sensitive. Use some of the following ideas to introduce some "new" foods into your diet. You of course should not eat any of the foods to which you have a sensitivity. For many people it is easier to approach dietary changes one meal at a time. As you prepare your meal, consider what substitute foods could be included in your diet. Write down these foods and the next time you purchase food, look for the available substitutes.

On rising

— a cup of warm water with fresh lemon (if not sensitive to citrus)

Breakfast

— multi-grain cereal; soy, rice, or nut milk; and a few nuts

— cooked grains: oat, millet, brown rice, amaranth, teff, quinoa

— cold cereal: puffed corn, puffed millet, puffed rice, brown rice, oat bran flakes, crispy oats, corn flakes, oatios, amaranth flakes, millet flakes with fruit juice or nut milk

— rice cakes with nut butter, fruit spread

— fresh fruit

— oat bran muffins

— buckwheat pancakes, waffles, french toast

— whole grain, rye or rice bread with fruit spread or

nut or seed butter (almond, sunflower, sesame)

— tofu scrambled with broccoli, peppers, onions

— butternut squash, yam or sweet potato with cinnamon

— herbal tea

Lunch

— fresh green leafy salad: 5 ingredients such as carrots, cabbage, beets, cucumbers, celery, peppers, tomatoes

— sandwiches: such as salmon, hummous, tofu, tempeh, mashed beans, poultry, nut butter, with romaine, chard, spinach, or sprouts

— soups: black bean, split pea, mushroom, barley, minestrone, french onion, miso with rice, potato chowder

— whole grain salad: barley, rice, quinoa, or millet with chopped vegetables (celery, carrot, peppers, cauliflower, zucchini, kale, chard, broccoli, shredded cabbage, parsley, etc.) and beans, fish or poultry

— raw vegetable sticks with crackers and dips, hummous (garbanzo bean spread), baba ganoush (eggplant), bean spread, guacamole

— tortillas filled with mashed beans, spinach, cucumber, sprouts, avocado, artichoke hearts, tomato, etc.

— large fruit salad

— herbal tea

Supper

— baked potato, yams, steamed vegetables, salad

— brown rice or millet, vegetable casserole or steamed vegetable, salad

— baked squash, legume casserole or soup

— broiled or poached fish (try different salsas to vary

the taste), whole grain (rice, quinoa, teff, etc.), salad

— poultry: cut in cubes and stir fry in water with garlic, onions, tomatoes, peppers, fresh vegetables, etc.

— whole grain pastas: use different varieties — quinoa, spelt, rice, spinach, corn etc., — with a variety of sauces: basil pesto, eggplant-red pepper, anchovy-caper, primavera (broccoli-mushroom, cauliflower, zucchini), pesto, walnuts, olives, etc.

— occasional omelet, with pesto, mushrooms, peppers, onions, olives, asparagus, salsas

— fritattas, a baked version of an omelet with more vegetables

— crepes with fillings: wild rice hazelnut, quinoa curry, salmon, mushrooms, etc.

— Mexican: bean burritos or tostadas with spinach. Spanish rice. Baked chips from corn tortillas with fresh salsa, chili

— stuffed yams, squash filled with falafel, whole grain salad with vegetables, nuts, tamari

— stir-fried vegetables, wild rice

— vegie burger, cooked vegetables or salad

Snacks

— air-popped popcorn with tamari, nutritional yeast, garlic powder, kelp, cayenne, or curry

— fresh fruit

— whole grain cookies

— whole grain pumpkin, zucchini bread

— rice cakes with nut butters, fruit spread, dips

— raw carrots, celery, peppers, cauliflower, broccoli etc.

— raw nuts and seeds; almonds, pumpkin, sunflower

Eating out

— soup & salad bar: avoid high-fat dressings, cheese, croutons, mayo, marinated vegetables

— pasta salad, ask for dressings on the side

— broiled fish with no butter

— baked potato with vegetable

Suggested Staples To Have On Hand

— variety of flours: amaranth, barley, brown rice, buckwheat, cornmeal, kamut, millet, oat, potato, quinoa, rye, spelt, teff, triticale

— variety of pastas: spelt, quinoa, rice, corn, artichoke, kamut, soba, spinach, Aglutella

— variety of pancake mixes: buckwheat, oat mix, brown rice, corn muffin

— organic pasta sauces

— olive oil: *extra virgin:* 1st pressing, very low heat (room temp); *virgin:* 2nd pressing; *pure:* high heat, chemical solvents, subsequent pressings of pulp and pits *(avoid!)*

— vinegar: rice, apple cider, herbal

— sun-dried tomatoes

— nut and seed butters (almond, cashew, sesame, sunflower)

— oil-free salad dressings

— soups: lentil, vegetable, tomato, split pea, black bean, potato, onion, etc.

— fresh vegetables (cut up and in a crisper in your refrigerator)

— fresh fruit (locally grown, in season, organic is preferred)

— fruit jams without added sugar or honey (Cascadian

Farm, Fairview, RW Knudsen, Westbrae brands)
— Garden burger (vegetables, brown rice, oats, wheat, parmesan)
— Ener-G egg replacer
— variety of convenience foods:
    vegetable or broccoli pot pie (Amy's)
    rice pilaf, hummous, tabouli (Casbah & Far East)
    instant refried beans, instant black beans, instant hummous, fantastic falafel, vegetarian chili, tofu burger (Fantastic foods)
    rizcous — lentil curry, vegetable chicken (Lundberg)
    ramen noodles — brown rice, onion, spinach (Westbrae)
— crackers, breads:
    corn tortillas, whole-wheat tortillas
    rice cakes
    Rye Krisp
    Wasa bread
    sprouted breads
    spelt bread, brown rice bread, rice potato bread, 4-grain bread
— for snacks: blue corn chips, brown rice chips, Kettle chips, black bean chips
— seasonings:
    herbs & spices
    tamari (natural soy sauce)
    pure vegetable seasonings (look for Vegit, Dr. Bronner's, Dr. Jenson's, Spike, Vegex)
    vegetarian soup stock
— beverages:
    herb teas
    soy milk (low fat vanilla, carob, plain)
    amazake, Rice Dream
    almond beverage, fresh nuts to make your own nut milk
    Cafix, Roma, Inka, Roastaroma, Postum, Caffree, etc.
    chlorine free water — bottled or filtered

Appendix Eleven

Milk

The following foods may contain milk in one form or another and should be avoided on a milk-free diet.

baker's bread

baking powder biscuits

bavarian cream

bisques

blanc mange

boiled salad dressings

bologna

butter

buttermilk

butter sauces

cakes

candies

cheeses of all types

chocolate or cocoa

chowders

cooked sausages

cookies

cream

creamed foods, sauces

curd

custards

doughnuts

flour mixes

foods fried in butter— fish, poultry, beef, pork

gravies

hamburgers

hot cakes

ice cream

malted milk

mashed potatoes

meat, commercially prepared— poultry, fish, luncheon

milk in any form; condensed, dry, evaporated, malted, powdered

oleomargarine

omelets

Ovaltine

Ovomalt

pie crusts (with milk products)

pizza

popcorn (with butter)

popovers

puddings

salad dressings

scrambled, escalloped dishes

sherbets

soda crackers

soufflés

soups— milk or cream

Spanish cream

spumoni

waffles

whey

whipped cream toppings

white sauce

yogurt

some "non dairy" products

"I always get a lot of mucus when I eat dairy products," is one of the common findings among my patients. This food group is responsible for almost as many different symptoms as MSG.

Otitis media (ear aches), excema, asthma, bedwetting, allergies, even juvenile onset diabetes has been implicated from dairy products which are given to children.

Gastrointestinal problems including bloating, flatulence, diarrhea, constipation are all suspect in patients who continue to consume dairy products.

Touted as the nearly perfect food (it is for baby cows), but very suspect for the human race. The increasing problems may be related to the increasing intervention in the lives and feed given to the cows. Hormones and antibiotics are now often routinely given with little to no research on the long term effects of these being added on the health of the humans who consume it.

With so many acceptable and better alternatives, let us shift our focus away from this group and instead towards other health building foods.

Milk-free Diet

Food Category	Foods You Can Eat, Unless Sensitive	Foods to Avoid
meat, poultry, fish, vegetable protein	veal, lamb, chicken, fish turkey, shellfish, dried beans and peas, nuts, nut butters	gravies and breading which contain milk, meat or fish fried in butter, cold cuts
dairy products	soy, nut, seed milks, margarine free of dairy, amazake; try West Soy Lite, Nancy's cultured soy (yogurt type treat), rice milk	whole, dry or evaporated milk, butter, cream, cheese, yogurt, margarine with dairy, ice cream, sherbet, cream substitutes with whey, lactose, casein
eggs	hard or soft cooked, fried, poached, scrambled	milk, cream or butter in cooking

grain products	cereals served with fruit juice or milk alternative, homemade bread without milk, bagels made with water, crackers made without milk, rice cakes	cereals served with milk or cream any bread with milk, waffles and other baked goods made with milk or milk solids
soups	soups made without milk, cream or cheese	soups with milk, cream, all canned cream soups
vegetables	fresh or frozen	all creamed vegetables, potatoes, covered with cheese sauce
fruit	fresh	
desserts	all that do not contain milk or milk products such as gelatin desserts, fruit	pudding and other desserts containing milk or milk products, whipped cream toppings, ice cream, sherbet, cake, cookies, prepared flour mixes
sweets		chocolate candy, candy
beverages	vegetable juice (fresh), herbal teas, mineral water, filtered water, unsweetened fruit juice, chicory and dandelion roots, Roma, Cafix, Inka, Roastaroma, Caffree	milk, milk shakes, hot drinks with milk added, cream, chocolate or cocoa made with milk
oils	olive, canola, flax, sesame, sunflower	

Appendix Twelve

Nuts And Seeds

"I never eat nuts and seeds because they contain too much fat," is a common comment from many of my patients.

Unfortunately, this is not a good idea. Nuts and seeds have a high protein content. They are rich in essential oils, vitamins and minerals for maintaining good health. Seeds should become part of your regular diet added to salads, as snacks or to dress up casseroles and healthy dressings. Adding a tablespoon two times a day will be a wonderful addition to your diet. Nuts provide a good energy boost when eaten in small amounts. They are excellent between-meal snacks, and can be added to casseroles and salads. Yes, they do contain fats so should only be eaten in small amounts.

Rancidity

Because nuts are rich in nutritious oils they become rancid quickly due to exposure to light, heat and air. Almonds are the most stable of all the nuts and keep well in a sealed container, but other nuts should generally be purchased in the shell and removed at the time of eating. At the very least, buy only whole nuts and chop or grind them at the time of use, as this will minimize their exposure to air and light and help ensure freshness. Store them in the refrigerator to minimize rancidity.

Purchasing nuts and seeds

When purchasing seeds such as pumpkin and sunflower, look for uniform color for freshness prior to purchasing. Flax, sesame and chia seeds are all stable until they are ground and then must be eaten immediately. Grinding the smaller seeds will help maximize their absorption, but they should be ground separately because of their differing consistencies. An inexpensive electric coffee grinder will work well and is easy to clean up.

(You won't be needing it to grind coffee beans anymore since by now you realize that coffee is not a part of good health building habits).

Flax, sesame, sunflower and pumpkin seeds are all rich in protein, minerals and the valuable essentials with:

* sesame and sunflower rich in calcium and linoleic acid (omega 6 precursor)

* flax rich in alpha-linolenic acid (omega 3 precursor)

* pumpkin seeds rich in zinc, iron, anti-parasitic enzymes and alpha-linolenic acid.

Comparing Nuts And Seeds

3½ ounce portion of	Calories	Protein (g)	Fat (g)	Percent of calories from:			
				Total fat	Saturated	Poly-unsat.	Mono-unsat.
Almonds	589	20	52	80%	8%	17%	52%
Brazil	656	14	66	91%	22%	33%	30%
Cashews	574	15	46	73%	14%	13%	42%
Chestnuts	245	3	2	8%	2%	3%	3%
Coconut	354	3	33	85%	76%	1%	3%
Filberts	632	13	63	89%	7%	9%	70%
Macadamias	702	8	74	95%	14%	1%	74%
Peanuts	567	26	50	78%	11%	25%	38%
Pecans	667	8	68	91%	7%	23%	57%
Pine nuts	515	24	51	89%	14%	37%	33%
Pistachios	577	21	48	75%	9%	11%	51%
Pumpkin	541	25	46	76%	15%	35%	23%
Sesame	573	18	50	78%	11%	35%	23%
Sunflower	570	23	50	78%	9%	52%	14%
Walnuts	607	24	57	84%	6%	55%	19%

Appendix Thirteen

Protein

Protein is one of the essential ingredients in our diet and it is necessary to make up at least 8-10% of the total calories we consume. Protein has many functions in the body, including forming structure in cells, antibodies, hormones, and enzymes. Proteins are composed of building blocks called amino acids, nine of which as considered essential.

Recommended daily allowance (RDA)

The recommended daily allowance is 56 grams for men and 44 grams for women. A pregnant or nursing mother would require a little more protein, up to 74 grams. A typical American diet is often closer to 100 grams of protein which is most likely too much and is not necessary.

Complete vs. incomplete protein

It was once considered necessary that all the essential amino acids be eaten at one meal. For vegetarians, this was especially considered important and they would combine beans and grains to obtain a "complete" protein. Studies have revealed, however, that this is not necessary and if you eat enough calories, you will most likely obtain enough of the essential amino acids. Amino acids are recycled by the body so even vegans who eat no animal products still receive all the essential amino acids.

Too much protein?

There are several conditions which require an increased protein intake. These include burn patients, malabsorption syndromes (such as celiac disease), ulcerative colitis, Crohn's disease, and a kidney condition where protein is lost in the urine.

Since this is not the situation for most people, they run the risk of eating too much protein. Studies have shown that too much protein may result in an increased risk of osteoporosis (thinning and weakening of the bones), kidney damage from the need to excrete excess nitrogen from the breakdown of the protein, and an increase in the risk of kidney stones because high protein increases calcium excretion in the urine.

A decreased protein intake is necessary in conditions of kidney failure, acute liver failure and patients with Parkinson's disease who are being treated with L-Dopa.

It is my suggestion that you try to obtain as much of your protein from non-animal products as possible. Non-animal proteins are associated with a lower risk of heart disease. The following table lists sources of protein and by using a variety of foods from the different groups, you will have no difficulty obtaining your daily requirement for protein.

Protein Content Of Foods

Food	Amount	Protein (grams)
Legumes		
beans	2 Tbsp.	6.1
chickpeas, garbanzo	2 Tbsp.	5.9
lentils	2 Tbsp.	6.5
lima beans	2 Tbsp.	7.1
peas	2 Tbsp.	6.7
soybeans	2 Tbsp.	9.9
soybean flour, low-fat	1 cup	45.1
soybean milk	½ cup	3.9
Seeds & Nuts		
brazil nuts	2 Tbsp.	4.1
coconut, fresh	2 Tbsp.	1.0
filberts	2 Tbsp.	3.6
peanuts	2 Tbsp.	7.6
peanut butter	1 Tbsp.	4.2
pecans	2 Tbsp.	2.7

sesame meal	2 Tbsp.	9.5
sunflower meal	2 Tbsp.	11.2

Grains

barley	2 Tbsp.	3.6
buckwheat flour, dark	1 cup	11.5
corn grits	1 cup	13.9
corn meal, whole	1 cup	10.9
oatmeal	1 cup	11.4
millet	2 Tbsp.	3.2
rice, white	1 cup	14.5
rye flour, light	1 cup	7.5
sorghum, grain	2 Tbsp.	3.1
wheat flour, whole grain	1 cup	16.0
wheat germ	1 cup	17.1
wheat macaroni, elbow	1 cup	15.7
wheat noodles	1 cup	9.2
shredded wheat	2 Tbsp.	2.9

Vegetables, Raw

cabbage	4 Tbsp.	0.8
carrots	4 Tbsp.	0.7
collards	4 Tbsp.	2.2
corn, sweet	4 Tbsp.	2.1
kale	4 Tbsp.	2.2
potatoes	4 Tbsp.	1.1
spinach	4 Tbsp.	1.3
turnip greens	4 Tbsp.	1.6

Meat, Poultry & Fish, Raw

beef, medium fat	½ cup	20.6
chicken, flesh only	½ cup	23.4
fish	½ cup	20.6
lamb, leg	½ cup	20.4
turkey, flesh only	½ cup	27.2
veal, round, boneless	½ cup	22.1

Milk & Milk Products

milk, cow, whole	1 cup	8.5
milk, goat	1 cup	8.1
milk, human	1 cup	3.4
cheese, cheddar	2 Tbsp.	7.1
cheese, cottage	2 Tbsp.	4.8
cheese, cream	2 Tbsp.	2.6

Eggs

whole, large	1 egg	6.4

Miscellaneous

gelatin	1 Tbsp.	8.6
yeast, brewer's	1 Tbsp.	3.0

Appendix Fourteen

Quinoa Recipes

Quinoa (The Basic Recipe)
Yields 4 cups

This light and wholesome grain may be prepared quickly and easily with this basic method.

2 cups water   1 cup quinoa

Rinse quinoa thoroughly, place quinoa and water in a 1½ quart sauce pan and bring to a boil. Reduce to a simmer, cover, and cook until all of the water is absorbed (10-15 minutes). You will know that the quinoa is done when all the grains have turned from white to transparent.

Quinoa (With A Gourmet Touch)
Yields 8 cups

Quinoa may be cooked as is or toasted. Toasted quinoa is light with a rich flavor. Quinoa is not enhanced when pressure cooked or cooked in cold water.

4 cups water   2 cups quinoa
⅛ to ¼ tsp. sea salt

Place water and sea salt in a 2 quart sauce pan and bring to a rapid boil. While water is heating place quinoa in wok or thin steel pan (cast iron is not advised) and, while stirring continuously with a wooden spoon, toast for about 10 minutes or until the color is a shade deeper and the quinoa emits a delicate fragrance. Add toasted quinoa to boiling water, cover, reduce to simmer and cook until all of the water is absorbed (15-20 minutes). Remove from stove and allow to sit 5-10 minutes before serving.

Variations: for a richer, nutty flavor toast quinoa in 1 teaspoon unrefined oil. For a heartier flavor sauté a pressed garlic clove and then toast the quinoa.

Buckwheat And Quinoa

4 cups water	1 cup unroasted buckwheat
1/8 to 1/4 tsp. sea salt	1 cup quinoa

Place the water and sea salt in a 1½ quart saucepan and bring to a boil. While water is heating, place buckwheat in a wok or skillet and toast, over a high flame while stirring constantly, until it turns a shade darker in color, about 10 minutes.

When water is boiling, add quinoa first and then add the buckwheat slowly or the water will bubble over the pot. Reduce the heat to low, cover and allow to simmer until all of the water is absorbed (15-20 minutes). Remove from heat and allow to stand for 5-10 minutes. With a damp wooden spoon, gently mix the grain from top to bottom while still in the pot. Cover again and allow to sit for 5-10 minutes before serving.

Tabooli
Serves 4

Tabooli, a mid-eastern salad made of bulgar wheat, is light, refreshing, and well suited to warm weather. Try it with quinoa for a delightful new taste.

2 cups quinoa, cooked	½ tsp. basil
1 cup chopped parsley	½ cup lemon juice
½ cup chopped scallions	½ cup olive oil

2 Tbsp. fresh mint or   sea salt and pepper
   1 tsp. dried mint
whole lettuce leaves   1 clove of garlic, pressed
¼ cup olives, sliced

Place all ingredients except lettuce and olives in a mixing bowl and toss together lightly. Chill for 1 hour or more to allow flavors to blend. Wash and dry lettuce leaves and use them to line a salad bowl. Add tabooli and garnish with olives. Serve.

Quinoa And Tomato Soup
Serves 6

1 Tbsp. unrefined oil   1 cup tomato, chopped
1 tsp. fresh cilantro   6 cups stock — chicken, fish,
   (coriander), minced   or vegetable
1 clove garlic, pressed   ½ cup quinoa
½ green pepper, chopped   2 stalks celery, chopped
1 onion, diced scallion   ¼ cup cheese, grated
   for garnish

Heat a 2-quart soup pot. Add oil and sauté cilantro, garlic, onion, pepper, celery, and then tomato. Add salt and pepper. Add stock and bring to a boil. Add quinoa and return to boil. Cover. Reduce heat and simmer for 45 minutes. Garnish each bowl with scallion and cheese. Serve hot.

Almond Cookies
Yields 1½ dozen

1 cup almond butter (tahini   ⅓ cup water
   or nut butter)   1 cup spelt flour
½ cup maple syrup or honey 1 cup quinoa flour

¼ cup unrefined sunflower ½ tsp. sea salt
  or safflower oil ½ cup toasted almonds,
1 Tbsp. vanilla   chopped
  9 whole almonds

Preheat oven to 375° F. In a small bowl blend almond butter, sweetener, oil and vanilla. Sift together flours and salt; add almonds and combine with almond butter mixture. Using your hands form into small cookies and place on an oiled cookie sheet. Press each cookie with the tines of a fork. Cut almonds in half and press one (cut side up) into each cookie. Bake for 12-15 minutes or just until browned.

Infant Cereal

As quinoa is high in protein, it makes an ideal infant cereal. The proportions for the recipe below yield a soft cereal ideal for a baby's first food besides breast milk. By increasing the water in the recipe below you can create a quinoa "milk" for bottle feeding.

¼ cup quinoa flour, toasted   1 cup water

Bring water to boil in a small sauce pan. Stir in flour with a whisk until smooth. Cover, place on a flame distributor and cook for 20 minutes.

Mediterranean Quinoa Salad
Serves 4

1 ¼ Tbsp. olive oil 1 garlic clove
6 mushrooms, minced 2½ cups cooked quinoa
3 scallions, minced ¼ tsp. sea salt
½ large red bell pepper, romaine lettuce leaves
  minced

Heat 2 teaspoons of the olive oil in a medium skillet over moderate heat. Add the mushrooms, scallions, red pepper, and garlic. Cook, stirring occasionally until softened, 2 to 3 minutes. Transfer to a serving bowl; add the cooked quinoa and toss with the remaining olive oil. Season with sea salt, then place in the refrigerator until chilled. To serve, line a plate with the romaine and mound the quinoa on top.

For a complete variety of 120 recipes, see: *Quinoa, The Supergrain*, Rebecca Wood, Japan Publications Inc., 1989.

Appendix Fifteen

Shopping List

Whole Grains
___ Amaranth
___ Barley
___ Brown/Wild Rice
___ Buckwheat
___ Cornmeal
___ Couscous
___ Kamut
___ Kasha
___ Millet
___ Oats
___ Quinoa
___ Spelt
___ Teff
___ Other

Pastas & Noodles
___ Amaranth
___ Buckwheat
___ Corn
___ Kamut
___ Quinoa
___ Rice
___ Rye
___ Soy
___ Spelt
___ Other

Breads
___ Multi Grain
___ Oat
___ Pita pocket
___ Rice
___ Rye
___ Spelt
___ Wheat-free
___ Yeast-free
___ Other

Flours & Powders
___ Almond Flour
___ Alum.-free Baking Powder
___ Alum.-free Cornstarch
___ Arrowroot Powder
___ Baking Soda
___ Barley Flour
___ Brown Rice Flour
___ Buckwheat Flour
___ Carob Powder
___ Cornmeal
___ Millet Flour
___ Oat Flour
___ Quinoa flour
___ Rice flour
___ Rye Flour
___ Soy Flour & Powder
___ Spelt Flour
___ Tapioca Flour
___ Whole-Grain Pancake Mix
___ Other

Dried Beans/Legumes
___ Adzuki
___ Black Turtle Beans
___ Black-eyed peas
___ Chickpea
___ Garbanzo
___ Kidney
___ Lentils
___ Lima
___ Mung
___ Navy
___ Pinto
___ Romano
___ Soya
___ Split Peas
___ Other

Nuts
___ Almonds
___ Brazil
___ Cashews
___ Hazelnuts
___ Pecans
___ Pine nuts
___ Pistachios

Seeds
___ Flax
___ Poppy
___ Pumpkin
___ Sesame
___ Sunflower
___ Other

Seed & Nut Butters
___ Almond Butter
___ Cashew Butter
___ Sunflower Seed
___ Tahini (Sesame Seed)
___ Other

Healthy Sweeteners
___ Apple Cider
___ Barley Malt Syrup
___ Brown Rice Syrup
___ Date Sugar
___ Pure Fruit Juices
___ Pure Maple Syrup
___ Stevia
___ Unpasteurized Honey
___ Other

Oils (unrefined)
___ Extra-virgin Olive Oil
___ Flax
___ Safflower
___ Sesame
___ Sunflower
___ Other

Salt And Salt Substitutes
___ Kelp
___ Sea Dulse
___ Sea Salt
___ Unbleached Rock Salt
___ Other

Fruits
___ Apple
___ Apricot
___ Bananas
___ Blackberries
___ Blueberries
___ Cantaloupe
___ Cherries
___ Cranberries
___ Fig (fresh)
___ Grapes
___ Honeydew melon
___ Huckleberries
___ Kiwi
___ Kumquat
___ Lemons
___ Loganberries
___ Mango
___ Marionberries
___ Mulberries
___ Nectarine
___ Papaya
___ Peach
___ Pear
___ Plums
___ Prunes
___ Watermelon

Unsulfured Dried Fruits
___ Apples
___ Apricots
___ Banana
___ Currants
___ Dates
___ Papaya
___ Pineapple
___ Raisins

Condiments
___ Apple Cider Vinegar
___ Cook Bag (herbs)
___ Dijon Mustard
___ Pure Vegetable Bouillon
___ Red Wine Vinegar
___ Rice Vinegar
___ Salsa
___ Soy Mayonnaise
___ Tomato Sauce
___ Wheat-free Tamari
___ Other

Vegetables
___ Asparagus
___ Beans (common)
___ Bok Choy
___ Broccoli
___ Cabbage
___ Cassava
___ Celery

___ Bamboo Shoots
___ Beet Tops
___ Broccoflower
___ Brussel Sprouts
___ Carrot
___ Cauliflower
___ Chinese Cabbage

Shopping List

___ Chinese Lettuce
___ Collards
___ Cucumber
___ Eggplant
___ Garlic
___ Jicama
___ Kohlrabi
___ Lettuce
___ Okra
___ Onions
___ Parsnips
___ Potato
___ Radish
___ Red leaf Chicory
___ Shallot
___ Sorrel
___ Squash
___ Taro
___ Turnip
___ Watercress

___ Chives
___ Cress
___ Dandelion Greens
___ Endive
___ Jerusalem Artichoke
___ Kale
___ Leeks
___ Mustard Greens
___ Olive
___ Parsley
___ Peppers
___ Pumpkin
___ Rutabaga
___ Sea vegetables
___ Snow Peas
___ Spinach
___ Swiss Chard
___ Tomato
___ Waterchestnut
___ Yam

Seasonings, Spices
___ Allspice
___ Anise
___ Bay Leaf
___ Basil
___ Caraway
___ Cardamon
___ Cayenne
___ Chicory
___ Cilantro
___ Cinnamon
___ Clove
___ Coriander
___ Cumin
___ Curry

Snacks
___ Apple Crisp Chips
___ Blue Corn Chips
___ Corn/Tortilla Chips
___ Fruit & Nut Bars
___ Ice Bean
___ Rice Cakes
___ Rice Dream
___ Whole-grain Cookies
___ Other

Beverages
___ Coffee Substitutes (Cafix, Caffree, Inca, Pero)
___ Herbal Tea (no caffeine)

___ Dill
___ Fennel
___ Fenugreek
___ Garlic
___ Ginger
___ Licorice
___ Marjoram
___ Miso
___ Nutmeg
___ Oregano
___ Parsley
___ Pepper
___ Rosemary
___ Saffron
___ Savory
___ Spearmint
___ Tarragon
___ Thyme
___ Turmeric
___ Other

Equipment
___ Blender
___ Coffee grinder
___ Grain Mill
___ Juicer
___ Steamer
___ Water Filter
___ Wok
___ Other

___ Pure Fruit Juice (Knudsen)
___ Natural Spritzer (Knudsen)
___ Other

Dairy Products
___ Almond Beverage
___ Rice Milk
___ Soy Milk (variety)
___ Almond Cheeze
___ Soy Cheese
___ Pacific Rice Non Dairy Drink

Healthier Flesh Foods
___ Cod
___ Halibut
___ Haddock
___ Ocean Char
___ Pacific Salmon
___ Pollock
___ Rainbow trout
___ Red Snapper
___ Rock cod
___ Rockfish
___ Sole
___ Wild Game
___ Free-range Chicken
___ Free-range Turkey
___ Other

Appendix Sixteen

Soy

Like corn, soy is found in a wide variety of foods. Careful label reading is essential if this important legume is among your intolerant foods.

Commonly used as an alternative formula for babies who are intolerant of milk products, it can create similar problems to the dairy it is replacing.

Bloody diarrhea, skin rashes, colic, ear infections, chronic skin rashes are among those symptoms that patients present with.

The following foods may contain soy and should be avoided on a soy-free diet. Note that soy is used as flour, oil, milk, and nuts.

Baked goods
some breads, rolls, cakes, pastries, packaged mixes
roasted soy nuts are used in place of peanuts

Sauces, dressings, oils

mayonnaise	salad dressings
lecithin spread	Crisco
miso	tamari
Worcestershire sauce	soy sauce

"vegetable oils" may contain soy oil (label may
   only say vegetable oil)
margarine, butter substitutes (note — Heartbeat
   margarine has no soy, but it is very low in
   cholesterol so it does not melt well when used in cooking.)

Cheese
processed cheese

Cereals, Pasta
boxed breakfast cereals (read labels)

soy flakes   soy noodles

macaroni   spaghetti

Beverages
soy milk— Mull Soy, Soyalac, Sobee

some bakeries may use soy instead of cow's milk

protein drinks   coffee substitutes (check label)

Meats
cold cuts   sausages

hot dogs   hamburger

hamburger extender   meat loaf

Vegetables
soy bean sprouts (especially in Chinese restaurants)

TVP (texturized vegetable protein)

tofu   bean curd

soy grits   natto

Desserts and candy
soy nuts are used instead of peanuts

hard candies   nut candies

caramels   chocolate

ice cream   sherbet

Other names for soy
lecithin (invariably derived from soybean)

emulsifiers   TVP

Appendix Seventeen

Spelt Recipes

Spelt is an easy digestible, gluten-containing grain. It is available as pastas (elbows, spaghetti, noodles), flour and whole spelt berries in your local stores or you can order directly from its distributor:

Purity Foods Inc.
2871 W. Jolly Road
Okemos, MI 48864-3547
(517) 351-9231

For persons who are wheat intolerant, spelt is easily substituted for wheat in recipes and offers a subtle nutty flavor. Because it contains gluten, it cannot be used by persons with a gluten intolerance. You can order a book called *The Wonderful World of Spelt* for $3.00 from this company which details the history of spelt and includes several recipes.

Spelt Hot Cereal

1 cup coarsely-ground spelt, spelt flakes or spelt farina
2 cups water   ⅛ tsp. sea salt

Combine ingredients in a saucepan, bring to boil and simmer 10-12 minutes. Stir occasionally. Serve with dairy substitute (soy, rice, nut, or seed milk) if you are milk intolerant.

Spelt Pancakes

2 cups spelt flour, coarse or fine	1 egg, optional
2 tsp. baking powder	3 Tbsp. oil
¼ tsp. sea salt	1¾ cup water *or*
1 Tbsp. maple syrup, optional	2 cups nut milk

Whisk together dry ingredients in a medium bowl. In a smaller bowl whisk together the liquids.

Preheat griddle. When a drop of water "dances" on it, pour liquids over flour mixture and stir to moisten. Oil griddle if not non-stick. Spoon batter onto griddle in 4-6 inch cakes. Turn when brown on one side and cook until second side browns. Serve at once with fruit topping.

Spelt Tortillas

1 cup spelt flour (+ ¼ cup for board)   ⅓ cup water
¼ tsp. sea salt   ½ -1 tsp. oil

Combine 1 cup of flour, sea salt, oil and water. Put remaining flour on bread board or counter top. Roll ball of dough in flour, flattening and folding the dough. In a few minutes you will feel the dough become more workable.

Divide into 4-6 small balls of dough. Working on the floured board, roll or pat each ball thin, to about 5-7 inches in diameter.

Heat griddle. When a drop of water "dances" on it, bake the tortillas about two minutes on each side, longer for crisper bread. Remove to wire racks and bake remaining tortillas.

Note: Don't limit tortillas to Mexican dishes. Tear one in the bottom of your salad bowl. Or spread thinly with sesame seed, cashew, almond butter. For the nut butter and jelly crowd, top with slices of banana.

Spelt Drop Biscuit

Preheat oven to 425° F

1 cup minus 2 Tbsp. tepid water	2 cups spelt flour
½ tsp. vitamin C crystals	½ tsp. sea salt
2 tsp. baking soda	3 Tbsp. oil

Combine the water and vitamin C crystals and set aside to dissolve. In a mixing bowl whisk together the flour, sea salt and soda.

When crystals dissolve, whisk in the oil and add all at once to the flour. Beat 10 strokes. Drop in mounds on a baking sheet. Bake 12 minutes until firm to touch and brown on the bottoms.

Spelt-Amazake Bread

6 cups spelt flour	3 cups amazake
½ tsp. sea salt	1¼ cup water
2-3 Tbsp. light sesame oil	1 cup of extra flour

Combine flour and salt, add oil and mix by rubbing between palms. Add amazake (room temperature) and mix well, then add water to form dough. Knead 300-350 times, adding flour as dough becomes sticky. Be sure dough is not sticky when you finish kneading. Divide dough in half, shape into loaves and press into well oiled bread pans. Make a 1" deep slit down center of each loaf. Cover pans with a damp towel, and put in a warm place for 8-12 hours.

Preheat oven to 300° F. Slit loaves again. Bake at 300° F for 20 minutes, then increase temperature to 350° F and bake for 1¼ hours. When done, bread should be golden brown and sound hollow when tapped at bottom.

Allow bread to cool in pans 10-15 minutes. Carefully remove. Allow to cool before slicing. Makes 2 loaves.

So you don't want to bake your bread by hand, then . . .

It is now easy and popular to make your own bread using a bread machine. This table-top appliance mixes and kneads the dough with a hook more powerful than hand kneading. It lets the bread rise and then bakes it, all in the same pot. There are several varieties available and the prices are reasonable. Examples of bread machines include Dak, Hitachi, Magic Mill, Maxim, Mr. Loaf, National, Panasonic, Regal, Sanyo, and Weldbilt. When baking with a bread machine it is very important to follow the directions exactly. You will not get good results if you don't measure your ingredients. Look for the book *Electric Bread*, Suzan Nightingale, Innovative Cooking Enterprises (I.C.E.), Inc., 1991, for tips and many great recipes.

If you wish to use a non-gluten flour, add one or all to your recipe: 1 tsp. vinegar, 2 tsp. xanthum gum, or more protein, such as eggs.

If the bread turns out too moist, use it for toast or rebake it in your conventional oven. Your experiments in adapting a recipe may provide you with lots of bread to put in the blender for bread crumbs (for your salads or stuffing for the turkey), but keep records. When you get the "right loaf," you can repeat the right combination.

Bread Machine, Spelt Recipe

(developed by Ginny Foster)

In a bowl, mix the following dry ingredients and allow to come to room temperature:

1 Tbsp. dry yeast in bottom of mixing pan (or whatever amount of yeast your machine recipes calls for)

2½ tsp. xanthan gum	1 cup spelt flour
½ cup rice flour	½ cup soy flour
½ tsp. sea salt	½ cup dry milk substitute

Mix the following wet ingredients and allow to come to room temperature:

1 tsp. vinegar	1 Tbsp. canola (or other oil)
2 Tbsp. honey	

2 eggs in a cup measure, fill to top with warm water, add 4 more Tbsp. water

Follow your bread machine directions for adding the wet and dry ingredients. Usually the recipe calls for dry first and then wet. Turn machine on and wait. If you like a soft crust, let the bread cool down in the machine.

Other recipes which can use spelt flour include:

saltines	muffins
yeast bread	dinner rolls
pita bread	carob cake
carob chip cookies	

Offer yourself an opportunity to use a different grain and experiment with some new recipes.

Appendix Eighteen

Sprouting

Advantages of sprouting

Seeds can be kept dry for many months or even years, and still be suitable for sprouting. The sprouting process accomplishes biologically what grinding does through the use of physical means, and what heating does through chemical changes. The chemical bonds for long term storage of nutrients are broken through the sprouting process, making them more easily available for use by the body. Additionally, there is the development of vitamins A, B, C, and chlorophyll. Sprouting is said to increase the content of B vitamins such as thiamin, riboflavin, niacin, pantothenic acid, pyridoxine, biotin, and folic acid.

Seeds to be sprouted

Any seed that will grow can be sprouted in a jar and used in cooking. A special favorite is alfalfa. Radish seeds, all the legumes, especially lentils, soybeans, and mung beans, are suitable for sprouting. Lettuce, radishes and similar plants that "go to seed" furnish good seeds for sprouting.

Uses for sprouts

In winter when greens are in short supply and are expensive in the market, sprouts can be prepared in the kitchen for use at a very inexpensive price. One can do one's own organic gardening in the kitchen. This kind of gardening requires no weed killing and no mulching. With judicious planning, sprouts can always be ready for use.

* Sprouts can be used separately with a little salad dressing or with other greens, tomatoes, celery, bell peppers, etc., as a tossed salad.

* Sprouts may be added to soups at the moment of serving.

* A favorite way to serve a thick vegetable stew is to float a large handful of sprouts on the top, and drop a dollop of mayonnaise on the mound.

* Sprouts may be liquefied in tomato juice or nut milk in the blender to make a delicious and nutritious beverage.

* Sprouts may be sprinkled on pumpkin pie for an unusual and crispy dessert.

* Sprouted wheat and sunflower seeds are good with fruits.

* Sprouts may be mixed in breads, using them whole or ground.

* Bean sprouts used as a main dish are very good as chow mein, burgers, or as cooked lentil or garbanzo sprouts.

* Soybean sprouts are especially good cooked as a main dish. The cooking time is greatly reduced (to about thirty minutes) for difficult-to-cook beans such as garbanzo and soybeans.

Method

The simplest method for preparing sprouts is by using a half-gallon jar with a jar ring and a wire screen or piece of sterilized nylon hose. Three tablespoons of whole, unsprayed seeds are placed in the half-gallon jar with a generous quantity of water (approximately 1 quart), to soak overnight. The next morning the seeds are rinsed well through the wire screen or nylon. The jar is turned upside-down to drain and then left with a kitchen towel covering the jar to make a dark place. The seeds should be rinsed twice daily through the wire screen (more frequently in summer to prevent the development of undesirable acids). Gently distribute the seeds around the sides of the jar by turning and shaking. The wet seeds will adhere to the jar wall. Sprouts are ready for use when one-fourth to one-half inch long. Alfalfa seeds can be allowed to develop the chlorophyll and vitamin A. Rinse in water to eliminate infertile seeds and hulls.

Seed	Comments	Use	Maturation (in days)	Vitamins Minerals
Adzuki Bean	mild, distinctive bean flavor, easy to sprout	salads, main dish	4-6	B1, B2, iron, potassium
Alfalfa	easy to sprout high in protein	mixed with cereals in bread, salads	5-6	C, D, E, K, phos., iron
Barley	more bitter in flavor than oats	cereals	3-5	B1, B2, C
Black-eyed Beans	good source of protein	useful in side dishes	3-5	B1, B3, C, iron
Buckwheat	taste varies with length	main dishes mix in bread	2-4	rutin
Chick-peas	good source of protein	salads, side dishes, cooked vegetable	5-8	B1, C, iron
Fenugreek	if too mature may be bitter	seasoning in salads	2-4	A, C, iron
Lentils	good source of protein	salads & side dishes	3-4	B1, B2, C, iron
Lima Beans	if oversoaked, they will ferment	salads	6	B1, B2, B3, C, iron
Millet	dried in oven used in bread	main dish, in cereals	3-5	B1, B2, C
Mung Bean	good source of protein, the longer the sprout, stronger the flavor	salads, side dishes	3-5	A, C, E, choline

Oats	pre-soak only 30-60 minutes	salads	3-5	B1, B2, C, iron
Radish	tangy taste	garnish or seasoning		A, B1, C, iron, phos.
Red Kidney Beans		main dish	3-6	B1, B2, B3, iron, phos., potassium
Rice	high nutritional value	salads, soups, main dish	3-5	B1, B2, C, iron
Rye	loses tenderness if grown too long	soups, salads	3-5	
Soy Bean	excellent protein	soy flour, bean soup, meat substitute	3-7	B, E
Sunflower	nutty flavor, use unhulled seed	polyunsaturated oil, salads	5-8	C, E
Triticale	fast growing	salads, soups	1-3	
Wheat	easy to sprout	salads, soups, ground for flour	4-6	

Appendix Nineteen

Sweeteners

People often choose sweets because they provide a pleasurable taste sensation. Man discovered honey bees and learned to cultivate sugar cane and sugar beets. There has been a continual search for a low-calorie or no-calorie substance which satisfies the taste sensation and is safe to eat.

There are over 200 chemicals known to taste sweet but many have problems such as a bitter aftertaste, lack of stability and toxicity.

Common sweetening agents include aspartame, fructose, glucose, mannitol, saccharin, sorbitol, stevioside, sucrose and xylitol.

Sucrose

To most people, sugar is sucrose, the white granular sweetener sold in bags at the supermarket. Although sucrose is widely distributed in nature in green plants, it is obtained commercially in large quantities from sugar beets and sugar cane.

The effects of eating sugar are widely known. There has been and continues to be a very divided debate as to whether children eating sugar have increased activity. The medical community continually cites studies saying there is no correlation between sugar and behavior.

Is sugar a cause for concern?

One very interesting study (Schoenthaler at el.) was conducted in the New York City public schools. A diet policy which lowered sucrose, synthetic food color/flavors and two preservatives (BHA and BHT) over four years in 803 public schools was followed by a 15.7% increase in academic percentile ranking above the rest of the nation's schools who used the same standardized tests. It is likely the improvement in performance can be related to eating less "empty calorie" foods and eating more nutrient dense foods.

How much sugar does the average person eat?

Since it is reported that the per capita consumption of refined sugar in the U.S. is well over 100 pounds per year, it is easy to understand all the health problems that are associated with empty calorie foods which contain a lot of sugar. I strongly urge you to substitute this product and those with names such as raw sugar, cane sugar, beet sugar, table sugar, brown sugar, cane molasses or turbinado sugar and use one of the natural sweeteners which are described below.

Natural Sweeteners

Natural sweeteners are delicious and if used in moderation they add a delightful dimension to life. Abused, they cause many of the same ills as other sweeteners.

Honey

Honey is the converted product of the nectar from flowers which is basically sucrose. Bees gather and break the sucrose down into the monosaccharides, glucose and fructose. These simple carbohydrates are called invert sugar. Honey contains 80% invert sugar. In processing for human consumption, honey is heated to filter out impurities. All truly natural honey is only heated to between 100°F and 145°F to preserve the natural enzymes, vitamins and pollen it contains. Raw honey is not heated at all or only to temperatures between 95°F and 105°F. Honey is rapidly absorbed into the bloodstream, immediately raising the blood-sugar level. As such, it is not a balanced sweetener. A balanced sweetener consists of a complex chain of sugar units which are broken off one at a time by digestive enzymes over a period of time. As it is being broken down, other important nutrients, such as protein, fat, vitamins and minerals are also being absorbed from foods.

The taste and color of honey is dependent upon the type of blossom it was gathered from. Honey has the highest sugar content of all the natural sweeteners and because it is high in fructose, it is one of the sweetest.

Natural honey is somewhat cloudy. The crystal clear purity of honey in the supermarket is obtained by heating the honey to very high temperatures and thus destroying the natural enzymes.

Maple syrup

Maple syrup is a naturally occurring sweetener, the mild flavor is unique, yet its sweetening ability is excellent. The reason for this is that 100% pure Grade A maple syrup is 65% sucrose. Lesser grades have a slightly lower sugar content. Maple syrup is sweet stuff indeed, and remember, when you pour it over your pancakes you are getting the equivalent of half that amount in white sugar. Like honey, it is quickly absorbed into the bloodstream, raising the blood-sugar level. It takes 40 gallons of sap from sugar maple trees to make one gallon of maple syrup, thus making it one of the most expensive sweeteners. When using this product make sure you buy "pure maple syrup" and not maple flavored syrup which is almost pure sucrose with a little maple flavor added.

Malt syrups

Malt syrups are made from cereal grains which are processed into syrup in the same way that enzymatic action in the mouth breaks them down when they are chewed. Malt is made from sprouted barley which is dried and powdered to be used in malting other grains. The malt is mixed with barley, rice, corn, or wheat and heated, which converts the available starches to sugar. The sugar contained in malt syrup is mainly maltose which is less than half as sweet as sucrose. Since it is not as sweet as other sweeteners, there is a tendency to use more. This is not a good idea since some malt syrups contain the same total sugar content as maple syrup. Malt syrups are still concentrated sugars.

Barley malt syrup

Barley malt syrup is less sweet than both molasses and honey, and on a fairly even par with brown rice syrup. High in complex carbohydrates, it enters the bloodstream slowly and can be considered a balanced sweetener, with less upset in blood-sugar levels. The malting process increases the level of B-vitamins in this product. It also contains some trace minerals.

Brown rice syrup

Brown rice syrup is a balanced sweetener. It is primarily a complex carbohydrate which enters the bloodstream more slowly than honey or maple syrup. Brown rice syrup doesn't contain as high a concentration of nutrients as does barley malt syrup, but it does contain some trace minerals and B-vitamins. It is less concentrated in flavor than other sweeteners and adds a mild, rather than a bold, sweetness.

Sorghum molasses

Sorghum molasses is made from a plant related to millet. The stalks of the plant are crushed, and the sweet syrup released is cooked and clarified into a dark syrup rich in minerals such as potassium, iron, calcium, and the B- vitamins. For this reason use sorghum molasses in place of cane molasses in any recipe. The sugar content of sorghum molasses is about 65% sucrose. Blackstrap and Barbados molasses are made from sugarcane.

Date sugar

Date sugar is ground from dehydrated dates and cannot be considered a sugar, but rather a food. It is high in fiber and rich in a wide range of vitamins and mineral, including iron. It does not dissolve, however, when added to liquids. Date sugar's most limiting factor is its high price.

Stevia

Stevia is a small wild shrub found in certain areas of South America. It is a plant of the chrysanthemum family. The sugars found in the leaf of the plant are 300 times sweeter than cane sugar. These sugars are called estevin and rebaudin.

One teaspoon of dried stevia leaves equals eight teaspoons of sugar. It may be used to sweeten hot or cold cereals, herbal teas and baked goods

There is some controversy in North America because stevia products are not approved for food use by the FDA even though they are accepted for general food use in Japan. The controversy stems from the fact that the stevioside, the sweet principle in stevia, is a glycoside, a molecule that is formed by joining a sugar molecule to another substance. In high doses, this compound may then have medicinal purposes. The effect of using high doses long term is unknown.

Fructose

Fructose is made in two ways. Most fructose is made by adding several industrial enzymes to corn syrup starch to produce sucrose. This sucrose is further broken down into glucose and fructose. Fructose is also made from refined cane or beet sugar which has the glucose-fructose bond broken. These forms should be avoided.

Fructose may be derived from natural sources such as fruits and vegetables, although it is more expensive to do so. Since it is not directly absorbed into the blood stream, it raises the blood sugar less dramatically which results in a smaller rise of the hormone insulin. Use this sweetener with caution as it may still be considered an overly refined product.

Upon examining all the sweeteners that are being marketed as natural, I suggest you avoid all of the following:

Corn syrup

Corn syrup is commercial glucose. It is made from corn-starch which is treated with sulfuric or hydrochloric acid, then neutralized and bleached with other chemicals. Everything but the starch is removed. Most corn syrup on the market is not pure, but has sugar (sucrose) syrup added since glucose is only about half as sweet as sucrose.

Aspartame

Aspartame (L-aspartyl-L-phenylanyl-methyl-ester) is a low-calorie sweetener used in foods and beverages and as a tabletop sweetener. It is sold under the name NutraSweet™ and Equal™ and is about 160 times sweeter than sugar with virtually no calories. The compound breaks down in our body to:

1. phenylalanine (50%) which can be neurotoxic and in some susceptible people can cause seizures,

2. aspartic acid (40%) which can cause brain damage in the developing brain, and

3. methanol (10%) which is metabolized to formaldehyde, an obvious toxin. Methanol is wood alcohol and is considered poisonous.

These all have adverse effects, but not everyone is affected equally. It must not be used by patients with phenylketonuria because of the release of phenylalanine during its metabolism.

Asparatame may cause a blockage of the formation of serotonin in the brain which makes people more susceptible to such things as insomnia, depression, hostility, anxiety and headaches.

One thirty-three year-old female presented to my office with a desire to lose weight. As a result of countless years of dieting using "low-fat, sugarless products" without success, she was also depressed. After eliminating her food sensitivities, which included aspartame in many diet products, she noted a dramatic improvement in her moods and also lost twelve pounds. Eating foods which the body tolerates can help establish a more biochemical balance which allows the loss of weight.

Many people use aspartame as a sugar substitute but most people who are sensitive to it will notice an increase in hunger pangs and so its use to consume less calories is offset by eating more foods. In a weight loss program this would prove to be futile.

The FDA position on aspartame

The FDA and Searle (the manufacturer of NutraSweet™) claim all symptoms are anecdotal and recommend that people see their physician for a diagnosis. This is in spite of the fact that "85% of all complaints registered with the Food and Drug Administration (FDA) concern aspartame's adverse reactions" as reported in the book *The Deadly Deception*.

What symptoms have been reported?

Headaches, nausea, vertigo, hearing loss, tinnitus, insomnia, numbness of extremities, slurred speech, mild to suicidal depression, personality changes, mood changes, anxiety attacks, hyperactivity, gastrointestinal disorders, seizures, skin lesions, muscle cramps, joint pain, fatigue, PMS, menstrual problems, chest pain, edema and increased appetite are but a few of the symptoms that have been reported.

Five deaths and at least seventy different symptoms have resulted from its use. The list includes neurological, dermatologic, cardiac, and respiratory symptoms. Aspartame may trigger or mimic many different conditions: chronic fatigue syndrome, Epstein-Barr, post-polio syndrome, Lyme disease, Meniere's disease, alzheimer's, epilepsy, multiple sclerosis and hypothyroidism.

Why would anyone even want to consider eating this proven unhealthy food? For your health, remove this "non-food" from your diet.

Problems related to this product are usually reported to start after a period of three weeks to a month from beginning its regular use. As a result, many people, including most physicians, do not recognize many of the above problems associated with this product and overlook it as the cause of their problem. Three of five negative responders have headaches and these are usually treated by recommending or prescribing some kind of pain killer, hardly the best solution to the problem.

Where do you find aspartame (NutraSweet™)?

Aspartame is sold to food processors for use in numerous products such as cold cereals, drink mixes, gelatin, puddings, dairy products, and toppings. It loses its sweetness during long periods of storage and is not suitable for baking since heat causes the loss of sweetness.

There are now more than 4000 products which contain this substance and television ads tell us that over 200 million people using it can't be wrong! It is used in more than 150 major brands of beverages, foods and other products in the following categories:

tabletop sweetener	powdered soft drinks
cocoa mix	puddings & pie fillings
topping mix	fruit juice drinks
yogurt-type products	instant coffee & tea mixes
shake mix	refrigerated tea
cereal	ready-to-eat gelatin
gelatin mix	chewing gum
instant breakfast mix	frozen desserts
frozen novelties	refrigerated flavored milk
milk flavor additives	beverages
wine coolers	breath mints
chewable	over-the-counter
multivitamins	pharmaceuticals

carbonated soft drinks   fruit syrups
fruit spreads & toppings

You should read *Aspartame (Nutrasweet): Is It Safe?* by H. J. Roberts, M. D. Charles Press, Philadelphia, 1990, $19.95. This book will alert you to the potential hazards of this sweetener. The book reports that aspartame may produce a wide variety of physical and mental symptoms which were listed above.

The Aspartame Consumer Safety Network (ACSN) serves as a support group and clearinghouse for information. You can write to them at PO Box 780634, Dallas, TX 75378. For $15.00 you can order *The Deadly Deception*.

Saccharin

This non-nutritive sweetener passes through the body unchanged and is excreted in the urine. A few studies have suggested it as being a suspected cancer causing agent.

It is widely used in beverages, jams, jellies, gelatin desserts, puddings, and salad dressings. Like NutraSweet, I do not recommend the use of this product.

Acesulfame-K

This product is sold under the brand names Sunette™ or Sweet One™ and was approved as a sugar substitute in 1988. It is used primarily in packet or tablet form. Like saccharin, laboratory tests have shown this product causes cancer in animals.

The manufacturer is seeking approval for use in soft drinks and baked goods but like the other artificial products, it has no place on the tables or in the foods of humans.

Reference

Schoenthaler S, Doraz W, Wakefield J. "The impact of a low-additive and sucrose diet on academic performance in 803 New York City public schools" *Int J Biosocial Research* 8(2); 185-195, 1986.

Appendix Twenty

Teff Recipes

Teff Breakfast Cereal

Here is a quick cooking cereal that is a great change from oatmeal and tastes good.

3 cups of water   1 cup teff

Bring water to a boil. Add teff, cover and simmer for 10-15 minutes or until the water is absorbed. Toward the end of cooking, stir occasionally. Serve with dairy substitute and maple syrup.

For a firmer cereal, cook in 2 cups of water. If you wish a smoother cereal, use 4 cups of water.

Teff Waffles

1¾ cups teff flour   2 tsp. baking powder
¼ tsp. sea salt   2 eggs, beaten
3 Tbsp. oil   1½ cups dairy substitute

Heat waffle iron. Into a mixing bowl, sift together flour, baking powder and sea salt. Make a hole in center of the sifted ingredients. Pour in liquid ingredients and stir with a few quick strokes, only enough to moisten the dry ingredients. (Batter will still have a pebbled look). Cook in hot waffle iron.

You may also decide to add 1 cup of blueberries or sliced bananas. Cook on a griddle for pancakes.

Basic Soup Or Stew

⅓ to ½ cup uncooked teff (or 1 to 1½ cups cooked teff)
¼ cup tamari soy sauce (not if sensitive to soy)
5 to 7 cups water   1 Tbsp. olive oil
1 large onion cut into thin slices   ½ head cabbage,
                                    shredded

Combine teff, water, and tamari in a deep sauce-pan; simmer. Heat a skillet. Add olive oil and onions. Sauté until onions begin to become clear. Add cabbage and sauté lightly. Add toasted sesame oil. Add vegetables to sauce pan. Simmer till done. Add herbs and pepper to taste if desired.

Teff Oat Bran Muffins

½ cup teff   ¼ cup boiling water
2 cups non-wheat flour   ½ cup oat bran
1½ tsp. baking soda   ½ cup honey (or equivalent)
2 Tbsp. oil   1 cup dairy substitute
1 egg, slightly beaten   1 Tbsp. orange rind

Preheat oven to 375° F. Oil muffin tin. In a mixing bowl, pour boiling water over teff. Stir to moisten all the teff. Set aside. In another mixing bowl mix flour, oat bran, and baking soda. When the teff mixture is cool, stir in sweetener, oil, dairy substitute, egg, and grated orange rind. Add to dry ingredients. Mix with a few quick strokes, spoon into prepared muffin tin and immediately place into preheated oven. Bake for 20 minutes. Cool for 10 minutes before removing from tin. Makes 12 muffins.

Teff Pudding

1 cup cooked and cooled teff 1 cup tofu
2-4 Tbsp. maple syrup 1 tsp. vanilla

In a blender combine tofu, maple syrup, and vanilla. Blend until smooth and light. Pour cooked teff mixture in a bowl. Mix thoroughly, cover and chill.

Variation: Add sliced bananas. Serve over teff-carob cookies.

Teff-Carob Cookies

¾ cup rice flour ¼ cup barley flour
1½ tsp. carob powder ¼ cup uncooked teff
¼ cup maple syrup ½ cup water
¼ tsp. almond extract

Mix dry ingredients. Mix liquids. Combine mixtures. Drop small spoonfuls onto oiled baking sheet. Bake at 350° F for 8-10 minutes.

Teff Flake Cookies

¾ cup oat flakes (rolled oats) ¾ cup non-wheat flour
¼ cup uncooked teff 1 tsp. baking powder
¼ tsp. sea salt 2 Tbsp. oil
1 egg, beaten ¼ cup honey or equiv.
½ cup dairy substitute 2 tsp. vanilla
¼ tsp. almond extract

Mix dry ingredients. Mix liquids. Combine mixtures. Let batter sit 2 minutes to absorb moisture. Drop by teaspoonfuls onto oiled baking sheet. Bake at 350° F for 8-10 minutes until edges are lightly browned. Cool.

Teff Burger

1 cup teff	3 cups water
1 tsp. thyme	2 cloves of garlic, minced
3 scallions, chopped	2 Tbsp. oil
lettuce, tomatoes	hamburger buns

Place teff, water, thyme, garlic in a pan and bring to a boil. Cover and simmer for 15 minutes. Stir once or twice toward the end of cooking. Spread cooked teff in a shallow pan to cool. When cooled, add scallions and form into patties. Heat a skillet, add oil, and fry until nicely browned. Turn over and cook till browned. Assemble burgers with lettuce and tomato.

Appendix Twenty-One

Wheat

The following foods may contain wheat and should be avoided on a wheat-free diet.

Beverages
ale, beer
cocomalt
gin (drinks containing grain)
neutral spirits
malted milk
Ovaltine
Postum
whiskey

Breads
biscuits
cornmeal muffins (commercial)
crackers
gluten bread
graham bread
hot breads
muffins
popovers
pretzels
pumpernickel bread
rolls
rye bread
spoon bread mixes
soy bread
Triscuits
white bread

Flours
baking powder (some)
buckwheat flour*
corn flour*
cornmeal (degermed, self-rising)*
gluten flour
graham flour
lima bean flour*
paten flour
rice flour*
rye flour*
white flour
whole wheat flour

Miscellaneous
au gratin potatoes
bologna
bouillon cubes
canned/instant soup
casseroles
chili con carne
chocolate candy
chocolate
cold cuts
cooked meat dishes
cooked sausages
creamed potatoes
cream soups

* not if you make the bread yourself using these flours.

Cereals

bran flakes
cornflakes
farina
Grapenuts
Krumbles
Muffets
Pep
Pettijohn's
puffed wheat
rice crispies
shredded wheat
malted cereals

Pastries and Desserts

cakes
candy bars
cookies
doughnuts
frozen pies
ice cream
pies
puddings
sherbets
sweet rolls
sauces
ice cream thickeners
salad dressings
synthetic pepper
vegetables prepared
  with sauce

Misc. (cont'd)

fish patties
fish rolled in flour
fowl rolled in flour
frankfurters (weiners)
fried veget. (floured)
gravies
griddle cakes
hamburger
hot cakes
ice cream cones
liverwurst
malt products
matzos
mayonnaise
meatloaf
meats rolled in flour
MSG
pancake mixtures
scalloped potatoes
soufflés
stuffing
swiss steak
timbales
vitamin E
Zest
wheat products
bread/cracker crumbs
dumplings
hamburger mix
macaroni mix
noodles
spaghetti
vermicelli
zwieback

Wheat-free Diet

Food Category	Foods You Can Eat, Unless Sensitive	Foods to Avoid
meat, poultry, fish, vegetable protein	veal, lamb, chicken, fish, turkey, shellfish, dried beans and peas, nuts, nut butters	any commercially prepared products with cereals: luncheon meats, frankfurters, meat loaf, sausage, meat or fish patties, casseroles with grain flour, canned or frozen foods with thickened sauces
dairy products	milk, butter, cheese, margarine, yogurt	milk drinks mixed with malt, cheese spreads with cereal fillers
eggs	hard or soft cooked, fried, poached, scrambled	eggs in grain-thickened sauces
grain products	barley, corn, oat, rice, rye, millet, buckwheat, quinoa, spelt, teff, wheat-free bread made from rice, potato starch, potato, lima bean flour, barley flour, millet flour, soy flour, oat flour, tapioca flour, quinoa flour, quinoa, corn, kamut, spelt pasta	wheat, wheat gluten, wheat flakes, wheat germ, shredded wheat, bulgur, wheat flour bread, dumplings, commercially prepared biscuits, pancakes, doughnuts, pastries, cakes, pies, pretzels, melba, toast, bread crumbs, croutons, noodles pasta, macaroni, spaghetti
soups	broth: homemade from allowed foods; creamed soup with potato thickener but not flour	bouillon cubes, commercially prepared soup thickened with wheat
vegetables	fresh or frozen	vegetables cooked with grain-thickened sauces
fruit	fresh	canned with grain-based

		thickening agents, fruit pies with wheat crust
desserts	gelatin desserts, rice or tapioca pudding, home-made ice cream, fruit ice or sherbet, custard	ice cream cones, cakes, cookies, pastries, prepared mixes, puddings thickened with wheat flour
sweets		chocolate candy, candy, molasses
beverages	vegetable juice (fresh), herbal teas, mineral water, filtered water, unsweetened fruit juice, chicory and dandelion roots, Roma, Cafix, Inka, Caffree, Roastaroma	coffee substitutes made with grains; instant beverages with malt or cereal added; beer, ale, whiskey, vodka, gin, lemon grass tea
condiments	salad dressings without grains, sea salt, pepper	commercial salad dressing thickened with grain, MSG
oils	olive, canola, flax sesame, sunflower	
miscellaneous	apple cider vinegar, wheat-free, corn-free baking powder	baking powder, chewing gum

Wheat-Free Recipes

Products made with non-wheat flours are usually heavy because the flours contain little or no gluten and are usually coarse so they need special handling. Gluten is a protein and is the substance in wheat that acts like glue and binds the mixture together. The non-wheat grains are coarse and heavy because it is difficult to grind them into a fine powder. Coarse flours do not readily absorb as much liquid as the soft flours. To improve the quality of non-wheat baked goods you should try:

* A gluten substitute — xanthan gum is the most satisfactory. You may also try guar gum, flax seed meal, eggs or egg replacer. If using xanthan gum, use 1 rounded teaspoon per cup of flour. It however does not mix well by hand so a rotary mixer, blender or food processor is necessary. You should keep xanthan gum in the freezer.

* Let the mixture stand for a period of time (several hours or overnight is ideal).

* Use smaller baking pans.

* Cook at a lower temperature and increase cooking time.

Basic Rice Bread

Be sure to read all the variations for this bread as it can be used in many ways.

2 eggs, separated	1 cup milk substitute
2 cups rice flour, sifted 3 times	1-2 Tbsp. honey
2 tsp. wheat-free baking powder	2 Tbsp. canola oil
½ tsp. sea salt	

Beat egg whites until stiff and set aside. In a bowl combine remaining ingredients, beating after each ingredient. Fold this mixture into stiffened egg whites. Pour into a well oiled and floured loaf pan. Bake at 350°F for 40-45 minutes or until done.

Variations:

1. Rice bread may be made without honey. Although a little more dry in texture, it can be moistened by serving with a fruit spread.

2. Make an herb bread by adding 2 Tbsp. chopped parsley and 2 Tbsp. chopped chives. Add any other combination of your favorite herbs.

3. For a dessert angel food cake, add 1 Tbsp. lemon juice and a little lemon rind. Serve as you would for a short cake with fruit and cream.

4. Double the recipe for angel food cake and bake in a large tube pan.

5. Basic rice bread can be baked as dinner muffins, dessert angel food cake or dessert muffins. Bake these at 350°F for 12-15 minutes.

6. Slice bread thinly and use in your french toast recipe.

Barley Bread

This bread can be used for a sandwich, toasted for breakfast or enjoyed as bread and butter. It may also be used as a base for bread crumbs, stuffing, and croutons.

2 cups barley flour	½ tsp. sea salt
2 tsp. wheat-free baking powder	⅓ cup powdered milk
1 tsp. honey (optional)	1 cup milk substitute
2 Tbsp. canola oil	

Combine first 4 ingredients and set aside. Mix together last 3 and add to the dry ingredients to form a soft dough. Flour hands and divide dough into 4 equal parts. Form into flat rounds on an oiled cookie sheet. Prick tops with fork. Bake at 350°F for 10 minutes. Cool and slice horizontally. It will make 2 thick slices or 4 thin slices.

Variation: Before baking, sprinkle top with sesame seeds.

Corn Bread

4 tsp. dry yeast	1 cup lukewarm water
1 cup cornmeal (yellow or white)	½ cup oat flour
¼ cup soy flour	¾ tsp. sea salt
2 Tbsp. honey	½ cup powdered milk
2 eggs, beaten	substitute
3 Tbsp. canola oil	2 Tbsp. nutritional yeast (optional)

Preheat oven to 350° F.

Dissolve dry yeast in lukewarm water and allow to stand 15 minutes. Combine in a mixing bowl: corn meal, oat and soy flours, powdered milk substitute, sea salt and nutritional yeast (if desired). Combine honey, oil and beaten eggs and add to dry ingredients, mixing well. Gradually add dissolved yeast mixture, blending well into other ingredients. Pour batter into a well-oiled (9 x 9 inch) square pan. Place pan in warm area and allow corn bread to rise 30-40 minutes. Bake in a preheated oven for 30-35 minutes.

Yield: 6-8 servings.

Millet Bread

⅔ cup millet flour	⅓ cup barley flour
1 cup grated raw carrots	1 Tbsp. honey
1 tsp. sea salt	2 Tbsp. canola oil
3 egg yolks	3 egg whites
¾ cup boiling water	

Preheat oven to 350° F.

Combine millet flour, barley flour, grated carrots, honey, sea salt and oil in a bowl; mix well. Gradually add the boiling water, mixing thoroughly. Beat egg yolks until light and lemon colored. Stir into the flour and carrot mixture. Beat egg whites until they peak, but are not dry. Fold carefully into batter. Oil 8 x 8 inch pan or 9 x 5 x 3 inch loaf pan. Line bottom with brown paper and oil again. Spoon mixture into prepared pan and bake for 30-40 minutes in preheated oven or until done. Remove from oven; set pan on wire rack and allow to cool for about 5 to 10 minutes. Remove from pan. Serve warm.

Yield: 5-6 servings.

Rye Bread

½ cup and 1 pint of water 3 Tbsp. yeast
1½ Tbsp. caraway seeds   2 tsp. sea salt
4 cups rye flour   ¼ cup canola oil
2 cups rye flour (more if needed for kneading)

Soak yeast in ½ cup lukewarm water and leave for 5 minutes. Make "sponge." Stir in 1 pint of lukewarm water, caraway seeds, sea salt and 4 cups of rye flour. Leave in a warm spot for 1½ hours, covered. Stir in oil and 2 more cups rye flour. Knead until smooth. Place in oiled bowl and let rise in a warm spot, covered, for about 2¼ hours, until double in bulk. Knead dough down, shape into round, high loaves (making 1 large or 2 smaller loaves), place on an oiled cookie sheets, cover and let rise in a warm spot for about 4 hours. Meanwhile, preheat oven to 350° F. Bake in preheated oven for about one hour or until done. Place a pan of hot water in the bottom of the oven to provide moisture during baking. Brush loaf with oil when loaf is removed from oven. Cool.

Yield: 1 large or 2 small round loaves.

Sweet Wheatless Bread
No-Knead Raisin Whole Grain bread

2 tsp. dry yeast	⅓ cup lukewarm water
2-3 Tbsp. honey	1¾ cup boiling water
2 tsp. sea salt	2 Tbsp. canola oil
1 cup brown rice flour	1 cup oat flour
1½ cup rye flour	1 tsp. cloves (optional)*
⅓ cup raisins (optional)*	

Dissolve dry yeast in ⅓ cup lukewarm water to which honey had been added. Combine boiling water, sea salt and oil in electric mixer bowl. Combine brown rice, oat and rye flours with spice and raisins (if using them) and add to boiling water mixture. Cool to lukewarm. Add yeast mixture and beat for 2-3 minutes. Cover bowl with damp cloth and set in larger bowl of hot water to rise for two hours. Beat dough again for 2-3 minutes. Turn dough into oiled 9 x 5 x 3 inch loaf pan and set in unheated oven to rise for 40-45 minutes or until it has just reached the top of the pan. Set oven at 400° F and leave it at that temperature for 10 minutes. Then turn heat down to 325° F and bake bread for 40-45 minutes longer. Turn loaf out of pan and cool on a rack before slicing.

*Note: Spice and raisins can be omitted for a plainer, but still delicious, loaf. For this, use 2 tablespoons of honey.

Yield: 1 loaf.

Pressure Cooked Bread

4 cups cooked grains	4 cups of flour (your choice)
2½ cups warm water	1 tsp. sea salt

Mix equal parts flour and leftover cooked grains. Vary grains according to season. Combine flour, sea salt and cooked grains. Mix together well before adding any extra liquid. Cover with a damp cloth and allow to rise in a warm place for 4-6 hours. Put rack in bottom of cooker and cover with 1" of water. Pour batter into a lightly oiled pan that fits in the pressure cooker. (Note that batter usually rises during cooking and can clog air vents). Place pan in pressure cooker, cover, bring water to a boil, and steam for 1-2 hours. Uncover and check that there is enough water in pressure cooker. Recover, place weight on top of cooker and bring to full pressure. Lower heat and pressure cook for 2 hours. Reduce pressure, remove bread pan from cooker and place on a rack to cool. (May look "globby" on top, but as it cools, moisture is reabsorbed into bread, giving it a pudding-like taste and texture). This is a rich bread that is very filling when eaten in small amounts. Is very satisfying and easy to digest. Good for lunches, on hikes, when traveling etc.

Optional items to add: leftover cooked vegetables, soba water (water left from cooking buckwheat soba noodles — it has a strong leavening power), cooked raisins, cinnamon etc.

Basic Muffins

1 cup oat flour	2 eggs
¾ cup barley flour	⅓ cup canola oil
¼ cup rice flour	¼ cup honey or maple syrup
3 tsp. baking powder	½ cup milk or water
½ tsp. baking soda	½ tsp. sea salt

Sift dry ingredients. Combine eggs, oil, honey and milk. Quickly stir in dry ingredients until moistened. Pour immediately into greased muffin tins. Bake at 375° F for 20-25 minutes. Makes 12 muffins.

Variations:

1. add ½ cup blueberries.

2. add ½ cup chopped cranberries.

3. add ½ cup well drained crushed pineapple.

4. add ½ cup chopped apples and ½ tsp. cinnamon.

Crepes I

These can be used for any occasion. Because of the natural sweet flavor of the rice flour, they can be served with just a fruit spread with breakfast.

2 eggs	½ cup rice flour
¾ cup milk substitute	⅛ tsp. sea salt
1 Tbsp. canola oil	

Combine all ingredients in a blender and blend until smooth. Heat skillet until water dances on surface. Spread 1 Tbsp. oil over surface. Pour 3 Tbsp. batter onto skillet tipping skillet in a circular motion to form a thin crepe. When brown, turn over to lightly brown the other side. Turn crepe onto paper towel to absorb excess oil and continue making other crepes. Remember the first crepe is usually a throw-away.

(You can freeze extras between wax paper and reheat when needed).

Crepes II

Makes approximately 12 large crepes

3 eggs	½ cup oat flour
½ cup milk substitute	¼ cup rice flour
½ cup water	½ tsp. sea salt
3 Tbsp. oil or melted butter	

Follow directions for crepe I

Buckwheat Pancakes

1 cup buckwheat flour	½ tsp. baking soda
1 cup oat or rice flour	2½ cups milk substitute
1 tsp. baking powder	¼ cup canola oil
¾ tsp. sea salt	2 beaten eggs

Combine first 5 ingredients in bowl and mix well. Add milk substitute, eggs, and oil; stir until smooth. Pour ¼ cup batter onto hot, lightly greased griddle. Cook until top is covered with bubbles and edges look cooked. Turn and brown other side.

Note: By using only half buckwheat flour, the taste is not so strong. Use them as a bread substitute and freeze them, two-at-a-time, in self-locking freezer bags, for use later in sandwiches.

Sweet Potato Buns

2 cups cooked mashed sweet potatoes or yams
1 tsp. oil   1 cup tapioca flour

Choose from the following for your filler

½ cup minced onion with   1 apple or pear, chopped
   2 Tbsp oil.   ½ cup nuts, chopped
½ cup raisins   4 plums, chopped
4 apricots, chopped   1 tsp. nutmeg (optional)

Add oil, tapioca flour and nutmeg to mashed sweet potatoes or yams. Mix the ingredients together, knead dough for 5 minutes. Break off pieces about 2" long and flatten slightly. Place a teaspoon of the filling of your choice in the center of each piece of dough and close by pinching the edges together. If using onions as your filler, sauté onions in 2 tablespoons oil before filling dough. Place on a greased baking sheet, bake for 30 minutes in a 300°F oven.

Yields 10 buns

Wheat Free Cake

1 ½ cups flour   3 Tbsp. carob powder
1 tsp. baking soda   ½ tsp. sea salt
½ cup canola oil   ¼ tsp. vanilla extract
1 cup apple juice or cider   nuts optional
or 1 cup apple butter and raisin puree mixture
½ cup soba water plus ½ cup cider

Thoroughly mix all dry ingredients together in a large bowl. In a separate bowl, combine all liquid ingredients. (When using soba water, let it ferment a day or two before making the cake. It is very leavening and makes a lighter cake). Add all liquid ingredients to the dry ingredients and mix well together. (An egg beater or electric beater will make a lighter cake.)

Bake in a preheated oven at 350° F for 30-45 minutes, or until it tests dry. Add roasted, chopped walnuts or filberts to the batter if desired. Dust nuts with flour first to prevent them from absorbing moisture during baking.

Add to an 8 inch square or round cake pan.

Popovers Or Yorkshire Pudding

½ cup rye flour   ¼ cup soy flour
¼ cup cornstarch   ½ tsp. sea salt
¼ cup soy milk powder   1 cup water
3 eggs, beaten   1 tsp. canola oil
3 Tbsp. oil for oiling pans

Preheat oven to 450° F.

Prepare muffin tin or 9 x 9 inch pan by coating the surface with oil. Place pan in preheated oven while preparing batter. Sift flours, cornstarch and salt into medium sized bowl. Combine soy milk powder and water with a wire whisk. Add beaten eggs, soy milk and 1 teaspoon oil; beat with rotary beater or wire whisk until batter is smooth. Pour batter into heated, prepared pan and place immediately in preheated oven. Bake 20- 25 minutes or until popovers have "popped" and are deep golden brown. Serve immediately.

Yields one dozen popovers.

Wheat-Free, Corn-Free Spaghetti

If you are a big spaghetti eater, stock up on spaghetti squash when in season, cook and freeze.

2 medium spaghetti squash   3 cups of your
                             favorite sauce

Cut squash in half lengthwise. Steam until tender (about 30-35 minutes).

Heat the sauce.

Remove squash from heat. Separate strands with a fork and remove from shell. Serve topped with generous scoops of sauce.

Serves four people.

Wheat-Free, Corn-Free Baking Powder

¾ cup cream of tartar   9 Tbsp. bicarbonate of soda
6 Tbsp. potato starch

Sift 3 times, mixing well each time. Store in airtight jar.

So you don't want to bake your bread by hand, then...

It is now easy and popular to make your own bread using a bread machine. This table-top appliance mixes and kneads the dough with a hook more powerful than hand kneading. It lets the bread rise and then bakes it, all in the same pot. There are several varieties available and the prices are reasonable. Examples of bread machines include Dak, Hitachi, Magic Mill, Maxim, Mr. Loaf, National, Panasonic, Regal, Sanyo, and Weldbilt. When baking with a bread machine it is very important to follow the directions exactly. You will not get good results if you don't measure your ingredients. Look for the book *Electric Bread,* Suzan Nightingale, Innovative Cooking Enterprises (I.C.E.), Inc., 1991 for tips and many great recipes.

There are many other books which have wheat-free recipes. Look for the following and others at the library or bookstore.

The Gluten-free Gourmet: Living Well Without Wheat, Bette Hagman, Henry Holt, 1990 ($22.50).

The No-Gluten Solution, The Cooking Guide For People Who Are Sick And Tired Of Being Sick And Tired, Pat Cassady Redjou, RAE Publications, 1990.

Appendix Twenty-Two

Yeast

The following foods may contain yeast and should be avoided on a yeast-free diet. Yeast is an additive ingredient in preparation (sometimes called "leavening")

baby foods
breads
cakes and cake mixes
canned refrigerator biscuits:
canned soups (some)
cereals fortified with thiamin,
   niacin, riboflavin, other
   vitamins
cookies
crackers

hamburger buns
hot dog buns
meat fried in cracker crumbs
milk fortified with vitamins
pastries
pretzels
rolls, homemade or canned
salt-rising bread
TV dinners
flour enriched with vitamins
   from yeast: General Mills

Yeast or yeast-like substances, because of their nature or method of manufacture, are also associated with the following foods and it may be necessary to avoid these also. You should ask your Naturopathic physician about your specific condition and his (her) recommendation.

apple vinegar
pear vinegar
grape vinegar
distilled vinegar, as such,
   or in catsup, pickles,
   horseradish, barbecue
   sauce, mince pie,
   mayonnaise, sauerkraut,
   french dressing, tomato
   sauce, Gerber's Oatmeal,
   olives, condiments,

barley cereal
whiskey, gin, rum, brandy,
   vodka, wine
all cheeses
sour cream
buttermilk
root beer
ginger ale
mushrooms
truffles

salad dressing
  chili peppers
cereals
candy
milk drinks that have
  been malted

soy sauce
citrus fruit juices, frozen,
  canned
dried fruits

Appendix Twenty-Three

Guide To Clean Air

The Environmental Protection Agency (EPA) has determined that indoor air pollution is a more consistent threat to your health than outdoor pollution. This pollution comes primarily from volatile organic chemicals such as formaldehyde, that are present in carpeting, paneling, cabinets, fabrics, and paint. (For a more complete list see environmental allergens, page 219). This pollution can be reduced with proper air filtration, certain plants or both.

Whether or not you have allergies to substances which circulate in the air, it is always wise to breathe the cleanest air you can. Your immune system can use any help you can give it.

There are numerous methods to recondition the air you breath daily. Depending on your personal situation and economics, it may be wise for you to consider one or more of the following filtration units and one or more of the suggested plants.

Humidifiers and dehumidifiers

People with respiratory problems usually feel better when they breathe moist air, as it keeps the nose and bronchial passages from drying out.

In the winter time when the heat is turned on, you may need a humidifier. Too-high humidity however, promotes the growth of house dust mites, molds, and fungi. In the summer, you may need a dehumidifier.

Indoor humidity of between 35-50% provides a balance between personal comfort and preventing growth of allergens. It is important to keep any units clean and mold-free by cleaning frequently.

Activated charcoal filters

Generally these filters seem able to absorb the fumes of cooking, cigarette and tobacco odors, gasoline fumes, smog and ozone, pet odors, and perfume. They are less effective against pollen, mildew, fish odor, and some noxious gases, and ineffective against carbon monoxide and formaldehyde. They may prove very helpful when used in conjunction with another type of filter.

Electronic air cleaners

The most common type of cleaner is the electrostatic precipitator. They work by drawing particles in, zapping them with an electric charge and then collecting the particles on a plate. This is supposed to remove the particles from the circulating air. Their effectiveness seems to vary and they may or may not prove helpful. The addition of a heat pump can further improve the air quality. Because heat pumps circulate more air, air passes through the filters more often and more particles are removed.

High efficiency particulate air filters (HEPA)

These filters seem to be very effective and remove pollens, molds, yeast, fungi, bacteria and viruses. If used with a charcoal filter, it can clean the air of large particles like dust and pollen as well as the minute chemical odors.

Air conditioning

This can definitely reduce pollen counts and also help with molds and dust-mites. Whether central or window mounted, they can help in two ways. They keep humidity low, which discourages mites and molds, and they can filter the air while cooling it. It is important to keep the coils and filters clean to prevent mold growth.

Negative ion generators

These replace positively charged ions (particles) with negative ions. The negative ions attach to contaminants, which then get attracted to walls, carpets, draperies, furniture and other surfaces closer to the ground and away from the air we breathe.

Table-top air purifiers

Most have a small fan which draws air through a filter and this may provide some degree of help in small areas.

Plants

The National Aeronautics and Space Administration (NASA) has done studies over the past decades to find plants which could remove toxic chemicals from the air of space stations. The plants they have recommended are:

Mass cane *(Dracaena massangeana)*
Pot mum *(Chrysanthemum morifolium)*
Gerbera daisy *(Gerbera jamesonii)*
Warnecki *(Dracaena deremensis "Warneckei")*
Ficus *(Ficus benjamina)*

Other plants effective for air purification are:
English Ivy *(Hedera helix)*
Marginata *(Dracaena marginata)*
Mother-in-laws tongue *(Sansevieria laurentii)*
Peace lily *(Spathiphyllum "Mauna Loa")*
Chinese Evergreen *(Algona "silver queen")*
Banana *(Musa oriana)*
Bamboo Palm *(Chamaedorea seifrizii)*
Heart Leaf philodendron *(Philodendron oxycardium)*
Green Spider Plant *(Chlorophytum elatum)*
Janet Craig *(Dracaena deremensis "Janet Craig")*

Once your system is working properly, it is important to remove the sources of pollution inside the home. Vacuum carpets and dust furniture frequently to get rid of unwanted pollutants.

Appendix Twenty-Four

Dust Allergies

People with dust sensitivity may notice they feel worse when the house is being cleaned, when the furnace comes on, in libraries, storerooms or other dusty areas, and when bedding is changed or the mattress is turned.

Plain ordinary house dust is one of the most common causes of allergy. It may contain numerous substances such as algae, bacteria, cosmetics, feathers, hair, house dust mites, insect particles, mold, plaster, pollen, skin scales, and anything else which may be floating in the air.

Common sites of exposure of dust include:

attic	chalk eraser	feed mill
broom	chicken coop	rugs
carpet sweeper	construction	toys
carpeting	drapes	vacuum cleaner
cellar	dusty books	floor rug
rec. rooms	book shelves	knickknacks
overstuffed furniture		stuffed animals

The most troublesome ingredient of house dust are the dust mites. These minute critters feed on flakes of skin which are normally shed every day. They love humidity, so bedding and upholstery in damp rooms set up an ideal living environment. The best way to control them is to control the moisture by using dehumidifiers.

The control of dust can seem like a never ending process because dust is everywhere. However, there is plenty you can do without being a full time cleaning person.

* Keep bedrooms to the bare essentials. Remove rugs and use only cotton curtains on the window. Wrap mattresses in a zipped, dust-proof cover. Synthetic pillows and mattress covers can be washed in hot water. Don't put items on top of dressers or put stuffed toys in the room. In the closet, clothes should be on hangers, not stacked on shelves. The entire room should be dusted daily, and wiped from top to bottom with a mop and damp cloth twice a week.

* Check filters on forced air heating systems. Many conventional furnace filters remove only 5-10% of the dust so you may cover all of the ducts with charcoal or washable cloth filters. The furnace should be vacuumed at least once a year, just before the heating season.

* Vacuuming regularly is important. Most conventional bag-equipped vacuums vent dust back into the air and are possibly one of the most hazardous appliances in the home. The smallest particles go right through the bag out into the air of the room. These extremely tiny particles of dust, mold and pollens then go very deep into the lungs. Central vacuum cleaning systems vent dust away from the area.

A more affordable solution is a water-trap vacuum cleaner. This model collects dust in water instead of an air bag, so the dust is not continually recycled into the air. In addition, it does not lose power like the air-bag models do when the bag fills up.

The very best type of appliance now seems to be a HEPA vacuum cleaner. The HEPA Nilfisk Allergy Vacuum Cleaner GS90 provides four stages of graduated filtration ending up with a HEPA filter which retains 99.97% of all particles down to 0.3 microns in size. The Vita-Vac™ is another type which also has a four-filter system.

* Buy stuffed toys which can be easily washed.

* Wear a dampened surgical mask when cleaning.

* Hang clothing in zippered garment bags. Place shoes and sweaters in compartmentalized areas.

* Throw out your carpets and buy throw rugs. Throw rugs can be washed at temperatures high enough to kill dust mites and the floor underneath stays cooler and drier, which also reduces mold growth.

* Avoid your food intolerances. This will enable you tolerate small exposures by reducing the total load of irritants on your system.

* Control dust in the bedroom. For many people the challenge of reducing your exposure to dust and its related elements can seem overwhelming. When starting to make changes in your home environment, I suggest you start in the bedroom with the following measures:

1. Encase pillows in zippered, dust-proof covers. Avoid feather and down pillows or comforters.

2. Encase the mattress and box spring in zippered, dust-proof encasing.

3. Remove all carpeting.

4. Avoid heavy curtains and venetian blinds, using window shades instead. If curtains are used, launder them frequently.

5. Use wooden or plastic furniture instead of upholstered furniture.

6. Wash linens and pillows in hot water regularly. Wash blankets in hot water every two weeks.

7. "HEPA" air cleaners can remove airborne dust particles.

8. Air conditioners can prevent the high heat and humidity which encourage mite growth. Use special filters to trap airborne allergens.

9. Cover hot-air vents with filters, or close the vents and use an electric heater.

10. Avoid wall hangings and other dust collectors.

11. Clean drawers and closets with a damp cloth. Wear a face mask when making the bed and doing housecleaning.

12. If using a humidifier in the winter, avoid too much humidity, as mites grow best at 75-85% humidity and

cannot live under 50%. Maintain around 35-40%.

13. Keep all clothes in the closet on hangers, not folded on shelves.

14. Keep pets out of the bedroom.

Appendix Twenty-Five

Environmental Allergens

Hair

cat	animal toys	caps
	earmuffs	imitation slippers
	gloves	rug pads
	cat skin and dander	
cattle	blankets	brushes
	rugs	rug pads
	cattle hair and skin	
dog	dog hair and skin	
horse	brushes	clothing
	gloves	hats
	mattresses	violin bows
	horse hair and skin	

Feathers

pillows	quilts, comforters
sleeping bags	parkas
household birds	farm birds

Wool

clothing fibers	wall-hangings
blankets	

Aspergillus

A type of mold that is found in many places

soil fungus	composts
damp hay	paper
fabric	leather
all grains	spoiled sausages
soya sauce	chocolate
cheeses	spices

Penicillinum

This is a dusty, blue-green mold, not the drug.
grows on fruit, breads, cheeses
fabrics, shoes, clothing etc.

Formaldehyde

This chemical is formed by the incomplete combustion of fossil fuels and is an air pollutant. It is used in the production of many home building products and is now considered an indoor pollutant. The most important exposures are from particle board and plywood, especially in mobile homes which are tightly constructed allowing for little air exchange with the outside. The effects of this chemical include nausea, vomiting, eye, nose, and throat irritation, and frequent respiratory infections. Infants are especially susceptible. It has been shown to cause cancer in laboratory studies.

particle board	plywood
synthetic resins	adhesives
plaster board	wood veneer
tanning agents	fertilizers
wallboard	chipboard
car exhaust	gas/oil combustion
air pollution	cigarette smoke
concrete	air deodorant
antiperspirant	antiseptic
dentifrice	shampoo

mouthwash	detergent
polishes	dyes
nail polish	preservative waxes
fabric stores	fabric fireproofing
paper products	wallpaper
insecticides	rodent poison
embalming fluids	photographic development

Chlorine

swimming pools	Clorox
bleaches	some insecticides
chlorinated drinking water	
detergents with bleaching agents	

Avoiding exposure

Some simple ideas to try and minimize your exposure to some of the common sources of environmental agents include:

* Allow good ventilation in all rooms.

* Use electric heat and appliances (vs. gas appliances).

* Use Castille or Ivory bar soap.

* Use Bon Ami, plain Dutch Cleanser, washing soda.

* Use Amway/Shaklee type laundry cleaning products.

* Air out dry cleaning articles before bringing in house.

* Use pump or roll-on products.

* Use white, unscented facial tissues, toilet paper and paper towels.

* Store foods in glass containers or cellophane wrap rather than plastic containers or wrap.

* Use natural fabrics like wool, silk, linen and cotton.

* Wash fabrics multiple times.

* Buy organic foods whenever possible.

Home cleaning kit

Five easily available ingredients — baking soda, salt, white vinegar, lemon juice and borax — will allow you to make your own home cleaning kit. With these products you can make cleaning products that are sometimes, although not always, as effective as commercial products but in all cases they are far safer and less expensive. This kit will reduce your family's exposure to cleaning chemicals like ammonia, phenol, chlorine, ethanol, cresol and lye.

* **Air freshener:** Sprinkle baking soda on the rug, leave a few minutes, then vacuum. This will help absorb food odors or musty smells.

* **Chrome polish:** Rub the chrome with newspaper or with white flour on a dry rag.

* **Drain opener:** Pour ½ cup white vinegar and ½ cup of baking soda in the drain. Cover tightly for 5 minutes and then rinse with hot water. Another method is to try ½ cup salt and ½ cup baking soda and rinse with hot water. While they may not be as effective as commercial products, they are far less toxic to your environment.

* **Furniture polish:** On a cloth place a mixture of equal parts of lemon juice and vegetable oil. Rub lightly.

* **Glass cleaner:** Mix ¼ cup of vinegar, 1 quart of water and a squeeze of lemon in a spray bottle and wipe with a newspaper for a very effective and ecologically safe method of cleaning your windows.

* **Linoleum floors:** Try ½ cup of vinegar in 1 gallon of water.

* **Mildew:** Wash the area with equal parts of vinegar and water.

222

* **Scouring powder:** Baking soda works to clean casserole dishes while borax and a soft brush helps clean porcelain sinks. Salt can be used to clean metal barbecue grills.

* **Spot remover:** Club soda applied immediately can remove most liquid stains. If the stain is set in, dab with undiluted lemon juice (after first testing color fabrics since lemon juice may bleach the product).

* **Flea Control:** Combine borax and baking soda, sprinkle into carpets, beds, couches, and sweep in with a broom. Let stand for 1-2 days and then vacuum. It may take more than 1 application but it will reduce or eliminate the need for foggers and sprayers.

* **Pesticides:** Try sprinkling borax, chili powder or pepper around areas where you see pests.

Appendix Twenty-Six

Mold and Mildew

Molds are a plant-like growth called fungi. Mold spores may be spread by the wind and cause allergies. Mildew is the black or white growth produced by mold spores. Garbage pails, shower curtains and damp basements are the most familiar mold habitats. However, any place that is damp, warm, dark and poorly ventilated is an ideal locale for mold. Mold is not only found indoors. Any place that harbors water — leaky pipes, faucets, sluggish drains, damp or flooded basements and crawl spaces — is an ideal home for mold. The following is a list of some common mold sites.

damp towels and clothing	old mattresses	refrigerator drip trays and door gaskets
foam rubber pillows	old, peeling wallpaper	potted plants
hay and grain fields	wallpaper paste	roof leaks into attics or behind walls
leather goods	overstuffed furniture	
old caulking around sinks and tubs	paint	vaporizers
woodpiles	pet litter	vegetable bins
	poorly vented closets	

Thus, it is important to control moisture in your house and surrounding environment. A good dehumidifier may be essential for those with mold allergies.

Typically mold is not strictly a seasonal problem, although it tends to flourish in the warmer months and diminish in the cooler months. A rainy summer may promote an excessive growth. Raking or burning leaves and mowing grass may stir up mold spores and cause allergy symptoms.

The antibiotic penicillin is a mold and people who have a penicillin allergy may also have a mold allergy. Conversely, those with a mold allergy may be allergic to penicillin.

Reducing mold and mildew

It is important that you do everything you can to reduce the amount of mold in your immediate environment. The following ideas may be helpful.

* Get rid of dampness. A wet basement may indicate cracks in the walls or inadequate drainage. Dehumidify a damp basement.

* Check your rain spouts. If your basement is damp after it rains, your down spouting may be placing the water too close to your foundation. You should then extend a spout to carry the water farther from the foundation.

* House plants may breed mold in their potting soil. Dried flowers may also contain mold. Allow your home to breathe by keeping the exterior of your home free of vines growing on the walls or shrubs and trees resting against the walls. Fallen leaves and piles of grass are also ideal spots for mold.

* Use light, washable throw rugs instead of heavy carpeting, especially in basements or other areas prone to dampness.

* Vent your clothes drier outdoors to help reduce excess moisture.

* Throw out old piles of odds and ends. Newspapers, books, old carpets, old furniture, dingy pillows and magazines.

* Keep things clean. Keep closets, dresser drawers, bathrooms and refrigerators as clean as possible.

* Spread out damp towels, washcloths and wet shower curtains. This would also include damp clothes, shoes and boots worn outside.

* Circulate the air. Use fans if there is no air movement.

* Sprinkle borax powder in mold-prone areas, like the bottom of garbage pails.

* Avoid wallpaper, especially in the bathroom. You may add

borax or boric acid to the paste to retard mold growth. Wash bathroom tiles frequently. Check corners, behind the toilet and under the sink.

* Use white vinegar or borax in warm water to clean mold surfaces such as the refrigerator door and rubber gasket and bathroom tiles.

* Avoid your food intolerances. This will enable you tolerate small exposures by reducing the total load of irritants on your system.

Some people may react to mold which is associated with certain foods. The following foods contain mold and may have to be eliminated or used with caution in cases of mold allergy:

— all cheeses, including cottage cheese, sharp ones such as blue and cheddar, sour cream, sour milk, buttermilk

— beer and wine, cider and homemade rootbeer

— mushrooms

— soy sauce

— canned tomatoes, unless homemade

— pickled and smoked fish and meats, including sausages, hot dogs, corned beef, pastrami

— vinegar and vinegar-containing foods, such as mayonnaise, pickles, pickled vegetables, green olives, sauerkraut

— soured breads, fresh rolls, coffee cakes, other foods made with large amounts of yeast

— all dried and candied fruits including raisins, apricots, dates, prunes, figs, melons, especially cantaloupe

Appendix Twenty-Seven

Pollen Allergies

Typically, pollen allergies have a definite seasonal pattern, usually worse in the spring and better in the winter. The pollen is carried everywhere by the wind (and sometimes by animals). Not all pollens cause allergies. Because their pollen is microscopic and easily carried by the wind, trees, grass and weeds are more likely to cause problems than flowers. Flowers produce large, sticky pollen which is carried by insects.

Pollen is usually worse on a dry, windy day and better when it rains. Levels are usually highest in the evening and early morning so staying indoors with windows closed may help you avoid the worst of it.

Several ideas to help minimize pollen exposure include:

* Air conditioning, both in your home and car, can reduce the need for open windows.

* Shower in the evening. This will reduce the pollens on your body and in your hair after being outside during the day. Otherwise, you may develop symptoms as the air conditioner circulates the pollen around the room while you are sleeping.

* Keep pets out of your bedroom. They carry pollen on their fur so minimize your exposure to them during pollen season.

* Keep your property well groomed. Remove any ragweed in the fall, consider ground cover with rocks and paths of crushed stone and other decorative ideas which could reduce the pollens in your yard.

* Keep dust and mold to a minimum. Avoid your food intolerances. This will often enable you to tolerate seasonal pollen allergies by reducing the total load of irritant substances you are exposed to.

Appendix Twenty-Eight
Booklist

There are *many* books which have substitutes, recipes, and other tips which will help you make the necessary changes. In a bookstore or library look at some of the books listed throughout the chapters or some of the following.

Food Intolerance, What Is It And How To Cope With It, Robert Buist, Prism Press, 1984.

Traditional Foods Are Your Best Medicines, Ronald Schmid ND, Ballantine Books, 1987.

Food Chemical Sensitivity, Robert Buist, Harper & Row, 1987.

If This Is Tuesday, It Must Be Chicken, Natalie Golos & Frances Golos, Keats Publishing Inc., 1983. (This book describes the basic principles of a rotation diet and gives menu ideas and recipes.)

The New York Times New Natural Foods Cookbook, Jean Hewitt, Avon Books, 1983.

The New Laurel's Kitchen, A Handbook For Vegetarian Cookery And Nutrition, Laurel Robertson, Carol Flinders, Bronwen Godfrey, Ten Speed Press, 1986.

Allergy Recipes, Sally Rockwell, Nutrition Survival Press, 1984. (Recipes are totally free of gluten, all grains — barley, buckwheat, corn, oats, millet, rice, rye, wheat — soy, peanuts, milk products, eggs, yeast, refined sugar).

Dr. Mandell's Allergy Free Cookbook, Fran Mandell, Pocket Books, 1981.

Freedom From Allergy Cookbook, Ron Greenberg, Blue Poppy Press, 1988.

The Allergy Self-Help Cookbook, Marjorie Hunt Jones, Rodale Books, 1984. (Contains 325 recipes free of wheat, milk, eggs, corn, yeast, sugar and other common food allergens.)

Discovering Natural Foods, Roy Bruder, Santa Barbara: Woodbridge Press, 1982.

Shoppers Guide To Natural Foods, East West Journal, New York: Avery Publishing Group, 1987.

Vegetarian Dishes From Around The World, Rose Elliot, New York: Pantheon Books, 1982.

Natural Foods Cookbook, Mary Estella, New York: Japan Publications, 1985.

Index

A

F

S

Symptom checklist 51-52
Symptoms, common with intolerance 4, 10

T

Tartrazine 136-137
Teff 68-69
  recipes 189-192
Thyroid problems 7
Tobacco 23-24
Trans-fatty acids 124
Triticale 69
Tyramine 38

U

Ulcerative colitis, and history of allergy shots 89
Urinary disturbances, as symptoms of intolerance 10

V

Vegetables
  directions for steaming 108
  introduction to baby's diet 33-35
Vegetarian milk recipe 75-76
Vomiting anecdote

W

Water 93
Wheat 69, 193-208
  hidden food sources 60, 193-196
  substitutes 70
  wheat free recipes 159-163, 171-175, 189-192, 197-208
  wheat-free diet 195-196
Withdrawal of offending foods 50-59
Wool allergens 219

Y

Yeast, hidden sources 209-210
Yellow dye #5 136-137

About the Author

Dr. Dick Thom graduated from the University of Toronto Dental School in 1974 and practiced dentistry in Eastern Canada until moving to Portland. He graduated from the Ontario College of Naturopathic Medicine in Toronto in 1986 and from the National College of Naturopathic Medicine in 1989. He presently has a full-time practice at the Beaverton Center for the Healing Arts in Beaverton, Oregon, and is an assistant professor at the National College of Naturopathic Medicine and a part-time clinic physician at the Portland Naturopathic clinic.

In his family medical practice, he has chosen to focus on the identification and management of food and environmental sensitivities, nutrition, homeopathy, and herbal and physical medicine.

The most important part of any practice should be education. After all, the word "doctor" is derived from the Latin word "to teach." Ultimately, patients are responsible for their own health and this book should be an aid in helping with the educational process.